Arup Associates Unified Design

Arup Associates Unified Design

Editor
Paul Brislin

Contributors
Gary Lawrence
Jonathan Glancey
Declan O'Carroll
Jay Merrick
Michael Beaven
Herbert Girardet
Juhani Pallasmaa
Leon van Schaik

John Wiley & Sons, Ltd

ISBN 9780470723319

Executive Commissioning Editor: Helen Castle
Development Editor: Mariangela Palazzi-Williams
Publishing Assistant: Calver Lezama

Book design and production: Arup Associates
Printed and bound by Conti Tipocolor, Italy

Contents

Foreword

Gary Lawrence

*Insanity is doing the same thing over and over again
and expecting different results.*

Albert Einstein (attributed)

As designers, too often we create the stage upon which the drama of life unfolds, without actually understanding the purpose of the play. As a society and as architectural practitioners we are not predisposed to take the time to explore projects laterally, to think about how the issue we are studying may relate to, or indeed even be caused by another, not on the table.

The world's complications are becoming clear: complications we have created for ourselves. Well intentioned but tunnel-visioned policy-makers and designers have spearheaded a descent into chaotic urbanisation. Ever more siloed thinking has led to the creation of transportation systems that do not consider land use, land-use regulations that do not account for energy needs, waste systems that fail to reintegrate wasted natural resources through recycling. We must embrace a new design paradigm wholeheartedly, efficiently and rapidly, before we squander our remaining natural resource capital.

The great civilisations of the past bequeathed us a legacy of iconic structures made by humans for human use. They were frequently engineering driven and beauty was seen through engineering eyes. In recent decades, however, the drive for the aesthetic has too often overwhelmed the need for utility.

On the other hand, the issues our society faces today are highly technical. Climate change is an accepted reality, although the specific consequences are still unknown. We are struggling to manage dwindling water supplies, inadequate electrical generation systems, rapid urbanisation and re-urbanisation, and demographic shifts. Our engineering expertise can easily seduce us into believing that solutions lie only in the scientific aspects of projects. Danger lies at the end of this path.

Gary Lawrence's views have been shaped by academic and professional practice, most profoundly through his experience as Seattle's Planning Director. He is Arup's Global Leader for Sustainable Urban Development.

7

The world cannot afford an overcorrection to the technical. The requirements of people, now and in the future, demand that we completely integrate not only aesthetic and scientific factors – but the real needs and desires of individuals: their senses, their emotions, their diverse identities too.

In a resource-constrained world – our world – a unified design approach is the most rational pathway to long-term value creation. Taken seriously, a unified approach requires us to address issues in depth, in breadth, at their intersections, and over time. Behavioural psychologists, sociologists, physicists, anthropologists, economists, public health officials: all need to be engaged in a broader definition of the design profession. Within this framework, unified design becomes the most robust way to seize opportunities. It also prevents any single interest from capturing the idea of 'design' and holding it hostage, impeding progress towards the ultimate goal: optimising conditions for sustained human development over an extended period of time.

If previous and current generations of designers are somehow complicit in the making of our present environmental and social conditions, then countering these conditions must surely require a radical shift in the way that we approach design. The world can no longer afford the folly of the disaggregated direction that design has taken in the past decade. It is now time to refocus on a unified approach, without which we stand very little chance of success. And when we do, people will no longer be extras to the set design – they will be liberated to become the playwrights too.

Introduction

Jonathan Glancey

Jonathan Glancey is an author and architectural correspondent for *The Guardian*, London.

Ludwig Mies van der Rohe suggested that architecture was 'the will of the epoch translated into space'.[1] More prosaically, and no less wisely, he also said architecture existed when two bricks were put together well.[2] His definitions are complementary rather than contradictory. This giant of early Modernism was right, yet only partially, as I'm sure he knew. Why? Because architecture, although a cultural continuum stretching back to the first temple complexes of ancient Mesopotamia, is an art, a discipline, a way of seeing and ordering the human experience, that continues to change.

Where once the story of architecture might easily have been read as the will of kings and priests, and later of energetic merchants, great landowners, industrialists and bankers, it has also been shaped and defined, and reshaped by teachers, philanthropists and doctors, by local authorities, by marketing, global branding and computer-era business corporations. This change is neither smooth, nor teleological, nor certain.

It moves in sudden shifts as well as with cultural, economic, technological and scientific undercurrents that, patchily charted, are not always understood even decades after their first appearance or discovery. And so, even while our cities – from London to Shanghai via Frankfurt and Dubai – continue to soar into the business-haven sky, and spread at the will of financially driven property development supported by governments of whatever nominal political hue, other concerns and developments are emerging to form new generations of buildings, new patterns of development, and to challenge those who design and create them. Today, the mid 20th-century definition of architecture as the 'crystallisation of capital in space', although telling, is only part of a bigger and increasingly complex picture.

It is true that we live in more fragmented times than ever before. The great civic structures of our own era are as much complex machines as they are works of art. Unlike Greek temples or Gothic cathedrals, contemporary buildings might look like anything, because they are not driven by beliefs, ritual, dogma or political certainties that nurture or drive them into particular forms, plans, sections and ways of commanding attention. This has proved to be a special challenge for architects. What should a new office block look like? Appearance matters. Even now, architecture is an art. Since the late 1990s, there has been a tendency to conceal such concerns behind what has been described as 'iconic' design, where form – the more exaggerated, simplistic and cartoon-like the better – triumphs over, and glibly conceals, every other concern.

This 'iconic' design is understandable. Marshall McLuhan saw it coming 40 years ago when he told us that 'the medium is the message',[3] and the 'medium is the massage', the title of his famous book published in 1967.[4] For better or worse, most of us live in a media-driven, marketing-formulated world, and much of our architecture expresses the sensationalism, the restlessness and the sheer neophiliac neurosis of a global culture given over increasingly to meaningless getting and spending. As all that's solid melts into the air, as Karl Marx predicted 150 years ago, especially in the age of global electronic communications, what should or can truly contemporary buildings, and cities, be?[5]

Significantly, Arup Associates was formed in 1963. The new practice was to be the niche vehicle that would deliver Sir Ove Arup's vision of holistic 'total design'. As Philip Dowson, a founding partner of Arup Associates put it, the aim of the practice was to develop 'an architecture derived from all the sources that can nourish it'.[6] For the current generation of Arup Associates' directors, this simply phrased yet complex concern is something that needs addressing anew. The primary aim is to ensure that new buildings truly take into account the ways in which the world, or our view of it, is changing.

Arup Associates' concern to nurture an environmentally, economically, socially and culturally sustainable future has been the driving force behind the concept of unified design. Unified design draws in every possible skill, discipline and way of thinking and seeing to develop buildings that are, as far as this is possible, seamless works of art, technology and science that, at the same time, are truly humane. Buildings that make people genuinely comfortable and at ease with themselves and their places of work, learning, entertainment, health, exercise and culture.

References

1   Ludwig Mies van der Rohe, quoted in John Zukowsky *Mies Reconsidered: His Career, Legacy, and Disciples*, The Art Institute of Chicago, Rizzoli International Publications (New York), 1986.

2   To be precise, Mies noted that 'Architecture starts when you carefully put two bricks together. There it begins.' Ludwig Mies van der Rohe, quoted in an interview, *New York Herald Tribune*, 28 June 1959.

3   Marshall Macluhan, *Understanding Media: The Extensions of Man*, McGraw-Hill (New York), 1964.

4   Marshall Macluhan, *The Medium is the Massage: An Inventory of Effects*, Bantam Books (New York), 1967.

5   Karl Marx and Friedrich Engels, *Manifesto of the Communist Party*, London, 1848.

6   Philip Dowson quoted in chapter on Dowson by Philip Manning, in Ann Lee Morgan and Colin Naylor (eds), *Contemporary Architects*, St James Press (Chicago & London), 2nd edn, 1987, p 243.

Teams of professionals and outsiders, where appropriate, consider all aspects of a building's design, its long-term sustainability. Each brief is approached from scratch to create buildings that are fit for our imagination and emotional as well as physical wellbeing. Buildings that will not follow a style or trend in design.

The design, and workings, of the extraordinary Druk White Lotus School set high on a mountain plateau at the Buddhist village of Shey in Ladakh contrasts with that of ultramodern studios for Sky in West London, due for completion in 2010, yet both projects are a part of the same holistic thinking. Both are responsible buildings, or building complexes, where the human element – what Arup Associates calls 'whole life sustainability' – comes first.

Arup Associates wants to learn, to hear from others as it researches and explores the architecture of coming years. Even this book is what its directors like to call a 'manifesto by example'. It is an opportunity to show what the practice has achieved in recent years, but more so, the book involves thinkers, writers and critics outside of Arup Associates. There is no certainty expressed in these pages, only an honest inquiry into what architecture and buildings might be as we move away from the era of gratuitous 'iconic' design. Here, in traditional book form, is an attempt at collaborative thinking and design.

Of course, this is a new beginning for a way of thinking that has been nurtured within Arup Associates for decades. Increasingly though, and with ever greater urgency, these are concerns that either do or will concern the majority of architectural practices in the long run. In the short term, however, brute economics, the seductive power of capital and our collective ego will continue to cultivate an architecture, and cities, of shiny grandeur that spell out irresponsibility and hubris in capital letters.

The Jesuit poet Gerard Manley Hopkins liked to say 'all my senses see'. Architecture is a visual medium, but as Juhani Pallasmaa stresses in this book, to be truly successful, truly humane, it must engage all our senses. And, as an overlapping current of these pages suggests, architecture must be sensible, an act of engagement in a world in which we have fresh concerns about ecology and the wider environment.

Architects have long spoken of 'responding to briefs' to shape buildings. Increasingly, they need to interpret and even to radicalise briefs, working with teams and individuals who can help clients think through what a building could be. This process of unified design is quietly ambitious – and a long, hard and fascinating road to tread. But, as this book suggests, here is a way of design thinking that needs framing afresh, and one that really does matter.

Part One defines unified design and demonstrates the sustainable agenda that is at the heart of Arup Associates' practice. **Declan O'Carroll** and **Jay Merrick** discuss design theory. A visual essay, **Plantation Lane** – a new collaborative architecture of memory and identity – provides an example of unified design in practice. **Michael Beaven** and **Herbert Girardet** consider the value of whole life sustainability, which is as much focused on the reprioritisation of culture and tradition as it is on radical new approaches to the environment and the reduction of energy consumption. Finally, a visual essay on **Vauxhall Transport Interchange** shows that extensive consultation and collective public opinion can still result in a distinctive public space. This project is a symbol of integrated sustainability and urban renewal, and a repository of new memories of transience and permanence.

ONE

UNIFIED THINKING

Unified thinking offers a radical alternative to conventional practice. It creates original design focused on people – their experiences, and their environment. It is entirely structured around a sustainable agenda.

In the contemporary world, design is a complex challenge. It requires unified collaboration: a wide and diverse partnership of people with specialist skills who know and respect each other, and share the same values and ambitions.

This is a time of change. We recognise the need to respond seriously to the emerging patterns that are redefining the world within which we live. Responsive design has the potential to transform the quality of people's whole life experience, offering solutions of intelligence and substance.

Unified Design:
A Radical Wholeness

Jay Merrick in conversation with Declan O'Carroll:

Arup Associates' vision of an architecture that addresses complexity and sustains humanity in the face of modernity

The pursuit of architecture in the 21st century puts its practitioners in vertiginous territory. Essential architectural reference points that once seemed usefully distinct – history, cultural norms, received notions of context and materiality – are today enmeshed and pixillated in the increasingly influential gravities of the virtual. We have never known so little about so many things. The machines we live in are not buildings, but macro-economic constructs. What are designers interpreting, and what can their architecture represent? Architects looking for meaningful points of response may sense something like the plummeting limbo of WB Yeats' tragic bird of prey:

> *Turning and turning in the widening gyre*
> *The falcon cannot hear the falconer;*
> *Things fall apart; the centre cannot hold;*
> *Mere anarchy is loosed upon the world,*
> *The blood-dimmed tide is loosed, and everywhere*
> *The ceremony of innocence is drowned;*
> *The best lack all conviction, while the worst*
> *Are full of passionate intensity.*
> *Surely some revelation is at hand…* [1]

What have Yeats' myth-misted cadences to do with unified design in architecture? For one thing, the verse reminds us that the 21st century's gyre – its vortex – is widening. Our perceptions and sense of existence, our thoughts, emotions and actions, are subject to increasingly disparate asymmetries: Google, YouTube, MySpace, Facebook, Wikipedia;

Jay Merrick is architecture critic of *The Independent*, London, and has written on architecture and art for publications including *Blueprint*, *New Statesman*, *The Architects' Journal*, *ArtReview* and *Art and Auction*. His novel, *Horse Latitudes*, was published by Fourth Estate in 2000.

Declan O'Carroll is an architect and a director of Arup Associates.

pathologically evasive ambiguity and irony; things that may be symbols, and symbols that may be things. Images, data and technology are only meaningful if they can be considered in wider, human relations; if they can't, they may seem mute and absurd, an effect that can be seen in the popularisation of architecture. The subject has been reduced: it's a Design/Designer thing, *whatever*. Architecture is too often implicated in both the Orwellian and Postmodern versions of Big Brother: it's entertainment, or the grist produced by wheels within wheels, rather than a thoughtfully presented expression of human and cultural presence. We are at risk of becoming supplicants to the iconic, and its Zen of architectural bling.

'Architecture is a human venture,' says an Arup Associates' director, Declan O'Carroll. 'We're looking at how to infuse a humble desire for the work to relate to people, and to carry an emotional resonance.' And he adds, influenced by the poet Seamus Heaney, that 'the minor exists in peoples' lives with the major. A simple, melancholic experience is as important to us as a grandiose experience.'[2]

The remark would resonate with architects who wish to engage specifically with humane, social or environmental issues. O'Carroll's comment lies in the shadow of increasingly brutal demographic, economic and cultural evidence. Mike Davis, author of *Planet of Slums*,[3] delivered a salutary drum-roll of statistics in 2006, and here are some bullet-points: by 2015, there will be 550 cities with at least 1 million inhabitants; by 2020, strip-cities will include a continuous 200-mile urban sprawl linking Accra in Ghana with the capital of Benin; within 50 years, 10 billion people, the bulk of the world's population, will live in the cities of developing countries; the two hypercities of Mexico City and Seoul, with populations of 20 million, will soon be equalled by São Paulo and Delhi. One sixth of the world's population already exists in so-called 'informal sectors' whose anarchic entrepreneurial and housing modes are beyond the effective reach of statutory or monetary regulation.

We are in a period of crucial urban and architectural experiment, or crude expediency, which in developed countries is based largely on the relationship between spending and supposedly verifiable outcomes. It now seems parodic to recall Mies van der Rohe's announcement of 'the spatially apprehended will of the epoch. Alive. Changing. New.'[4] In 1932, at about the same time as Mies' Dalek-like declamation, Aldous Huxley's negative utopia, *Brave New World*, clearly foresaw that the will of the Modernist epoch would veer towards rationality, diagram and the allure of *Technik*. More than eight decades after these seminal visions, today's architectural 'revelations' have tended towards hyperbole,

Above
Hypercity: Mexico City

via architects of strongly technological or sculptural inclination. Blatantly virtuosic demonstrations of technical refinement, or formal sensationalism, are producing buildings as mysterious as sub-atomic quarks; this is architecture as a bulwark against doubt, or the risk of wider cultural engagement.

The timing of Arup Associates' development of unified design, following successive iterations of the integrated design processes pioneered in the 1960s, reflects the increasing complexity of cities, in particular their greater cultural diversity, their infrastructural and transport herniations, the remorseless demand for housing on sites of increasing difficulty, and the evolution of radically *laissez-faire* education environments. These ingredients seem, on occasion, to be caught up in the slipstream of that most ubiquitous of displacement activities: consumption. And in this mall-like ambience, design processes are tainted by a mysterious sense of velocity; the result is an expression of human erosion, or perhaps simple survival, rather than fertility.

'Many of the problems we witness in the world today are a result of design decisions,' says O'Carroll. 'This is not limited to the field of architecture. We are forming an over-indulgence on technology to solve our problems, many of which have been created by not recognising the impact of technology in the first place.' That impact was identified in a particularly resonant manner by the philosopher Martin Heidegger in 1959, in a speech relating to his book, *Discourse on Thinking*.[5] He suggested that the 'releasement toward things and openness to the mystery belong together. They grant us the possibility of dwelling in the world in a totally different way. They promise us a new ground and foundation upon which we can stand and endure in the world of technology without being imperilled by it.'

The impact of technology is partly rooted in the selective clarity of Modernist photography, which has been dominated by what Susan Sontag described as 'the savage autonomy of the detail.'[6] And O'Carroll believes that 'our era is image-dominated like no other. This has been reinforced through technological invasion. The dominance of vision is apparent everywhere. The manifestation of the image, and the ever-developing modes of transmission, are saturating us. We are now able, through ordinary technology, to see simultaneously into all corners of the globe. Consequently, our experience of space and time has become diffused and confused. The visual image has become an experience commodity. Our natural inner construction of reality has become disorientated, resulting in a crisis of representation. The authentic difference between image and reality has become increasingly blurred. We seem to readily accept the image as being equally representative and authentic as reality itself. A contemporary culture which prioritises the visual image over reality diminishes our other perceptual characteristics. Our other senses are becoming desensitised.'

The attractions of High-Tech architecture or wilful formal abstraction are not surprising, nor always utterly craven. They are individualised, more or less omniscient reactions to client expectations, and to the way architecture and urban development is perceived as a commodifying process, rather than a holistic response. Most often what is called for is either value-engineered architectural and functional clarity or, if the budget allows, something deliberately extraordinary. The press tends to react by emphasising architectural extremes, the 'Wow' factor. Their coverage is reductive and veers between, say, dazzling High-Tech buildings in Kazakhstan or Kuala Lumpur and houses made of carpet tiles or old car tyres, designed and built by Rural Studio in Alabama. Freakish (and visually striking) architectural extremes are the general requirement. Very little popular critical recognition is afforded to how buildings actually perform. Architectural uniqueness is lionised; information about whole life building performance, or how buildings have affected lives, is generally deemed superfluous.

This reductionism, among both commentators and architects, threatens to disable progressive, inclusive debate about design processes. The profession risks losing any sense of an inter-dependent, usefully volatile, condition of enquiry from which new modes of design response can evolve; a common place of ideas and actions, as it were, inhabited primarily by humane motives and, secondly, by certain highly sensitive relations of expertise designed to express and communicate those motives.

What is the nature of this common place, this potential start-point, in architecture? In the face of an exponential array of alluring start-points, what kind of primary intentionality best suits design processes in the 21st century? In championing architects of hermeneutic persuasion, the celebrated historian and architectural commentator Dalibor Vesely has coined the term 'grey zone'[7] in approval of those architects whose work springs from a relatively complex mulch of contextual and cultural considerations: Alvaro Siza and Alvar Aalto are examples of grey-zoners, and there is no doubt about the contextually considerate, humane and engaging power of their architecture.

Layers of phenomena – some of them significant, most of them random and unintelligible – inform architectural reactions in the 21st century. The key issue isn't that architects must

Above
Window detail, Arup Campus, Solihull, 2007:
cedar cladding, timber-framed glazing and *brise-soleil*

develop an encyclopaedic understanding of phenomena or contextual narratives in order to develop design intelligently (though this may help). A fundamental position of reaction is required from which the details of the world, and architectural projects, can be assessed and weighed. That fundamental position may not, of course, be about architecture, as such. What if it is about something else, something pre-tectonic; something very basic and open-handed?

'Architecture requires us constantly to reinterpret and revalue technology in human and social terms,' wrote Philip Dowson in a 1980 publication, *Contemporary Architects*.[8] His conviction was that 'close-knit, interdisciplinary design teams were necessary to confront the scale and complexity of modern buildings if an architecture is to survive which embodies humane ideas… However, whilst method and analysis can never substitute for an architecture which helps to enrich and not diminish our lives and surroundings, nevertheless, in considering means and ends, the ends have become so complex that it has become necessary to design new ways of designing new buildings, if an architecture is to be derived from all the sources that can nourish it.' In 2004, in *Architecture in the Age of Divided Representation*, Dalibor Vesely warned that architecture-as-instrument has generated a mosaic of expert knowledge, brought together as abstract technical systems, which obscure the full possibilities of architecture.[9]

Dowson and Vesely's views were expressed even more directly by Hugo Häring who, in 1925, dissociated himself from the prefigured rationalism of Le Corbusier's Five Points by declaring: 'We want to examine things and allow them to discover their own forms. It goes against the grain with us to bestow a form on them from the outside, to determine them from without, to force upon them laws of any kind, to dictate to them.'[10] Four years later, Eileen Gray was even blunter: 'It's always the same story: technology ends up as the principal preoccupation. The end is forgotten by only thinking of the means… we must build for people so that they can find once more in architecture the joy of enlarged powers and self-fulfillment.'[11]

In these resonant remarks, we see that Arup Associates' 21st-century quest to establish a unified design ethos – a self-levelling compass in the widening phenomenological uncertainty, as it were – carries the genetic markers for practice set out 37 years ago by Dowson. Today, we might query certain dynamics in Sir Philip's remarks – notably, his implication that in the face of increasing architectural complexity the way to reduce inhumane effects is to apply cross-fertilised intelligence to projects capable of 'creating an environment for mass need '. There is a tension between this Modernist instinct to design

UNIFIED PRINCIPLES

Unified design is a radical, pan-disciplinary, collaborative approach to architecture that focuses on people-oriented design from the outset, through the unified vision of architects, engineers, artists, sculptors and social scientists and others

Unified design delivers a holistic architecture driven by a sustainable agenda

Designs must achieve whole life sustainability, which reaches beyond obvious notions of energy saving, to maintain culture and tradition through a reprioritisation of the importance of human experience, the senses and memory

Whole life sustainability places people first. It enhances the cultural value systems found within different locations, rather than creating modernist models that expect people, cities and places around the world to behave in identical ways

Design must evolve from the users' perspective, at human scale, both for the individual and the community

Design solutions are always generated from fundamental research and experiential goals – from the inside out – and are never imposed by the requirements of external image alone

Optimum solutions are found through exploratory parallel studies

There are no standardised solutions for any particular site, context or use

There is no predetermined visual 'style': each project finds its own unique expression

Unified design centres on an imperative to discover rich and subtle environments that respond to all the senses

Unified design develops a mode of creativity that is more than simply the sum of the individual disciplines. Instead, when boundaries are blurred, the very process of design maximises the potential of collective creativity

for mass need (with its peculiar suggestion of a singular object) and the idea that the way to do it is to absorb 'all the sources that can nourish it'. That tension remains – quite properly – in the practice's current ambitions for unified design. But Dowson's credo has developed into a new language of engagement and interpretation based on individual rather than mass need. Declan O'Carroll's metaphors and references not only reflect our phenomena-saturated times, but are field-maximising tools that establish a mindset of inclusion, more effective tessellations of individual responses, and make allowance for unpredictable design possibilities.

Thus, unified design requires more than certain valuable core design skills embedded in a single practice. It seeks a radical, pan-disciplinary approach that is implicitly outward-looking. Instead of absorbing 'all the sources that can nourish it' in an intelligent but essentially passive way, the new dynamic will bring those sources into design processes: various kinds of artist, social scientist, cultural commentator – anyone who can enrich design at an early stage, make it more responsive and humanely ambitious before form and structure are defined. The human, physical experience of buildings is seen as crucial. Tectonics, spatial atmospheres, materiality, programmes and aesthetics are regarded as realms in which the senses, memory and imagination of individuals are enlivened, rather than progressively deadened.

O'Carroll emphasises that the unified design of architecture is, as he puts it, people-orientated, a process that 'works from the inside, out, through multiple parallel studies, to find a solution that is never driven by image alone. Our approach to design is one that attempts to sustain all the components of humanity, and concerns itself with sustaining individual lives in a holistic way.'

'We're not talking simply about reducing energy consumption. We believe the real issue is how human culture – tradition, religion, joy, pain, and the intangible components of humanity – can be sustained in the face of modernity. Architects and engineers – and their clients – have to find new ways to judge what's required – and deliver it. I believe we must, increasingly, prioritise the needs of individuals. We must remember that architecture is for people, and that the thing people most want to do is live fully engaged lives. And, at the root of that desire and challenge, lies the need to re-prioritise the importance of the details of human experience by communicating and enriching the physical, the sensual, the imaginative, and the contextual.'

In considering Arup Associates' new direction, it is interesting to look back on their earlier projects in the 1970s and '80s. One finds a powerful diagrammatic and elevational clarity, and little formal or material brutality. And one sees an intriguing displacement of subtle architectural creativity. The practice's architecture in that period was both tough (Harold Wilson's 'white heat of technology' still echoed) and artistic, in a measured way. The mediating human touch was found in the detail. Consider the understated elegance of the slim arcade columns and shallow arches below the Vaughan Building at Somerville College, Oxford; or the vertically striated bricks at Ampleforth College; or the concrete handrail mounts at the CEGB Regional Headquarters near Bristol; or the engrossing mixed materiality of the entrance at Leckhampton House at Corpus Christi, Oxford. Buildings like these suggest permanence, certainty, dates carved into cornerstones.

But the past and future, as ideas or conditions to engage with, are increasingly fugitive. What place has unified design in the 21st-century event-horizon? What might it be? Unified design is an architectural process which seeks to heighten the quality and human worth of inter-disciplinary reactions and outcomes. At a more fundamental and hazardous level, it is a design process that – regardless of the scale or function of the brief – seeks a direct unification or fusion with an even more important process: *living*.

'The domain of architecture is unique amongst the arts,' says O'Carroll. 'It carries a greater burden of direct responsibility. Unlike the traditional domains of other arts, where the relationship of engagement is by choice and consent, architecture is by its nature omniscient. It can be unforgiving in its impact on people. Our modes of creation should be cognisant of this responsibility. No other art has the ability to directly enhance the quality of people lives; and no other has the capacity to inflict as much misery.'

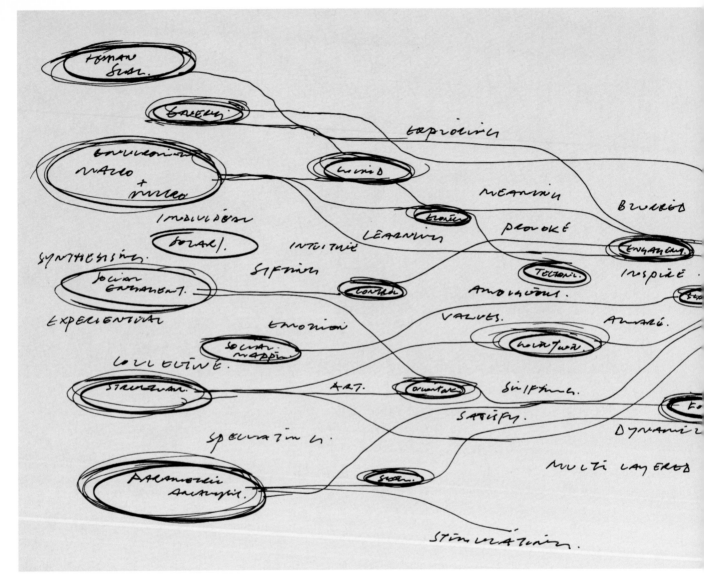

Above
Arup Associates: unified thinking, speculative and multi-layered

O'Carroll cites the role of contemporary novelists in describing the sense of our whole life experiences. Writers often articulate a world which we recognise our universal need for diversity and richness, to sustain a fulfilling life experience where the complex and simple exist side-by-side, and create a sustainable balance. It is this dynamic which satisfies the diversity which we need to feed our whole life experience.

'Our built environment is inextricably linked to our sense of self. It acts as a key influence in the quality of our whole life experience. Indeed, as a backdrop to support diversity of experience it is entirely natural that this manifests itself in an array of different and often contradictory ways. This *bricolage* of environments is in harmony with the diversity that feeds our whole life experience. This complexity contrasts with the key influences directing many contemporary architectural creative methodologies, which are overly simplistic in

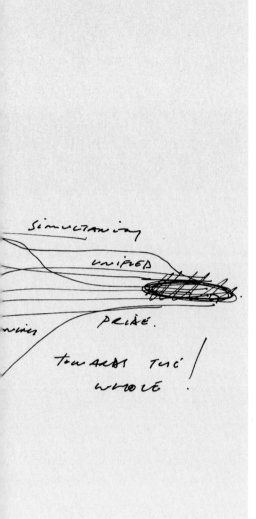

comparison. They are impoverished of subtlety; they are pathologically fleet-footed and innovative. They reveal a disproportionate obsession with developing a signature style, independent of other conditions.'

And those other conditions are fundamentally of sensual origin, says O'Carroll: 'Our engagement with architecture is dependent on the senses; it is empty of meaning and relevance without the interaction of people. It is only through the senses that architecture comes to life and exerts its full potential. Our senses integrate our experience of the world. Our architecture needs to rediscover its potential to stimulate all the senses.'

The last sentence is of particular interest. It is an admission that architecture – even ostensibly engaging architecture – may be in the process of becoming a kind of wallpaper, a barely noticed stage-set; as mute and tragic as the small city of packing crates in the closing scenes of *Citizen Kane*. But it is also an ambitious challenge to find new ways to make architecture significant to people – not just functionally or programmatically, but as a field of recognitions; architecture as a fact, but whose moral and communicative value transcends its factuality.

'We're suggesting the *opposite* of a unified language of architecture,' O'Carroll explains. 'We want to go beyond the classic western scientific model of breaking things down to their smallest parts and re-assembling them. If you take a complex form, reflect it in a mirror, and then smash the mirror, you only see part of the whole in a shard. In a hologram, a shard reveals the whole image, the whole complexity.[12] What we're interested in, through unified design, is not about the Miesian idea of the god in the detail. Part of our desire is a level of honesty in the way we articulate this message. For example, I don't think there can be any such thing as a finished idea – or essay, for that matter. And very few clients want to accept that. They want guidance, to give them confidence in their investments.'

Arup Associates' quest for engaging, humane architecture requires design processes that may be based on unfamiliar scenarios; on ideas and research drawn, as O'Carroll puts it, from a kind of peripheral vision where unexpected contextual or interpretive possibilities are noticed: 'We have to be inventive enough to capture the speed of change.' For example, in developing a conceptual framework for the Sky Campus at Hounslow – which will have a population of 8,000 – Arup Associates used a behavioural psychologist to assess campus cultural values, and spatial perceptions.

'No bubble-diagrams or adjacencies,' O'Carroll muses. 'Instead, organisational ideograms and mental mapping.' A kind of complexity theory is being embraced. In the case of Sky's broadcasting headquarters, 10 versions of the building were devised and interrogated, along with sub-variants. The practice's research unit is now, as a matter of course, using interactive designer–client spatialisation and visualisation software; and programs designed to reveal unexpected information about organisations that could usefully inform conceptual reactions and refined design. The research unit also spends time assessing the crossover potential of innovations in non-architectural fields. More is more.

Arup Associates is proposing a unified design ethos that will require its architects and consultants to engender ideas via a kind of personal primal gestalt process in which the usual grammars and codes of architectural discussion will not, initially, be mandatory. Unified design is a commitment to intensely omnivorous research into the very processes of project development and their potential qualities as a communicable human experience. This gives unified design philosophical credentials – removing it, for example, from the strictly positivist-cum-determinist canons of Modernism.

'If elements of experimentation and research cannot exist outside of their own reality,' says O'Carroll, 'then their overall contribution is limited, and compromised. The focus of the next generation of pan-disciplinary collaborative partnerships will be in generating new creative techniques and methods to unify the whole. Unified design develops a method of creativity that is more than the sum of individual disciplines. Instead, the boundaries are blurred, and the very process of design maximises the potential of collective creativity.' And if this mantra produces buildings and spaces of recognition and participation rather than terminal autonomy in the 21st century, Arup Associates will have revivified Philip Dowson's prescient vision of an 'architecture derived from all the sources that can nourish it.'[13]

This essay was developed through a series of conversations between Jay Merrick and Declan O'Carroll that took place during September 2007.

References

1 'The Second Coming', WB Yeats, *Collected Poems,* Everyman's Library (London), 1921.

2 Seamus Heaney, *The Redress of Poetry*, Farrar Straus and Giroux (New York), 1996.

3 Mike Davis, *Planet of Slums*, Verso Books (New York and London), 2006 in Jeremy Harding, 'It Migrates to Them', *London Review of Books*, 8 March 2007.

4 Mies van der Rohe in Ulrich Conrads, *Programmes and Manifestoes on Twentieth-Century Architecture*, printed as part of 'Working Theses', 1923, with the translation: 'Architecture is the will of the age conceived in spatial terms. Living. Changing. New.'

5 Johann Heinrich Heidegger, *Gelassenheit*, Vittorio Klostermann (Frankfurt), 1959, vol 16 of the *Gesamtausgabe*, HarperCollins (as Harper Perennial) (London), 1969.

6 Susan Sontag, *At the Same Time: Essays and Speeches by Susan Sontag*, Farrar Straus and Giroux (New York), 2007 in Jenny Diski, 'Seriously Uncool', *London Review of Books*, 22 March 2007.

7 Dalibor Vesely, in *Eric Parry Architects 1*, Black Dog Publishing (London), 2002.

8 Philip Dowson quoted in chapter on Dowson by Philip Manning, in Ann Lee Morgan and Colin Naylor (eds), *Contemporary Architects*, St James Press (Chicago & London), 2nd edn, 1987.

9 Dalibor Vesely, *Architecture in the Age of Divided Representation*, MIT Press (Cambridge MA), 2004.

10 Hugo Häring, *Wege zur Form*, October 1925.

11 Eileen Gray, 'From Eclecticism to Doubt', *L'Architecture Vivante*, Autumn 1929, p 20 in Colin St John Wilson, *The Other Tradition of Modern Architecture*, Black Dog Publishing (London), 2007.

12 Henri Bortoft, *The Wholeness of Nature: Goethe's Way of Science*, Floris Books (Edinburgh), 1996.

13 Dowson, op cit.

Plantation Lane:
Time and Tide

Arup Associates: Dialogue with Memory

Plantation Lane: Time and Tide
Dialogue with Memory

Above
Inlaid limestone, set in 'Univers 55 Oblique'

Left
View to St Margaret Pattens' Church

Twisted alleyways have always been the connective tissue of the City. Plantation Lane is a newly formed pathway that carves through an entire London block, from Wren's Church of St Margaret Pattens to Mincing Lane. It weaves two recent buildings by Arup Associates into the fabric of the ancient capital, and provides opportunity for a unique 21st-century medieval alley.

Unified design rejects the application of a globalised 'signature language', independent of context and culture. Instead, an often speculative and lateral process is followed, to find forms and materials rooted in their surroundings. The language emerges directly and sometimes surprisingly from the site. Here, above 2,000 years of Roman and medieval London, Arup Associates has explored a contemporary experience grounded in local memory.

The search for independence from any pre-established architectural language and a desire for a place-rooted physical and emotional depth sparked the conceptual theme: a counterpoise of text and image, stone and light. The first pair engages with memory; the second with the senses. In modern European cities the traditional role of written text – of marking territory, of celebrating influential people and important events – has been lost. To re-establish this territorial marking Arup Associates deliberately set up a duel between the physical and the immaterial: a confrontation between historically reverberant words cut deep into the granite ground plane, and the 21st-century resonance of an illuminated screen. The screen, 41 metres long and 6 metres high, sharply defines the pedestrian route and creates an unobstructed vista to St Margaret Pattens' Church spire. It is a transient painting in colour and light, disconnected from the earth to reinforce its 'other-worldliness' – a counterfoil to the tactile traditional craft of inlaid stone beneath.

Within our design studio, experimentation with form and material – the 'sifting' of ideas – is a fluid process. Essential to unified design is the parallel collaborative involvement of others, such as artists, in the development of the work. Orthodox boundaries that separate disciplines are deliberately removed. Our intent at Plantation Lane was to challenge the limitations of traditional public art, which so often concludes in 'object making', independent of context and place. Crucially, here, the artwork was developed hand-in-hand with the design of the new public space, rather than commissioned separately. Simon Patterson, 1996 Turner Prize nominee, was a natural partner. His body of work reflects an interest in the combination of visual and textual references. It was clear that he shared our ambition to use evocative language and imagery to celebrate the unique history of the site.

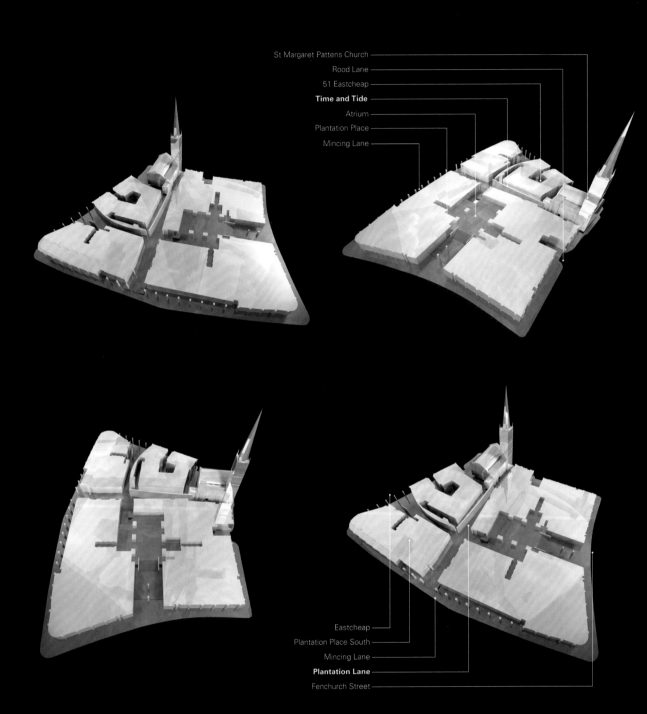

St Margaret Pattens Church
Rood Lane
51 Eastcheap
Time and Tide
Atrium
Plantation Place
Mincing Lane

Eastcheap
Plantation Place South
Mincing Lane
Plantation Lane
Fenchurch Street

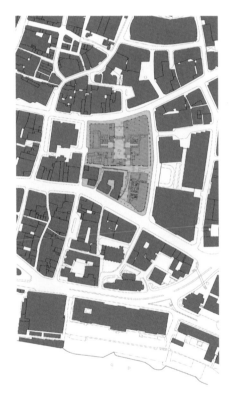

Patterson conceived an image of the moon to suggest constancy during times of change, and as a counterpoint to the difficult, rapid and often violent transformations that have imposed themselves upon the people of London. Patterson also devised the collection of texts inset into the stone pavement. The limestone letters sit along a series of great arcs, which slide underneath the mass of the new buildings adjacent. Each curve represents a different timeline that begins with Roman gods and goddesses, and moves through a range of evocative and idiosyncratic miscellania: from the City Guilds; hidden rivers; streets of carnal knowledge; plagues and disasters; to the hierarchical membership degrees of the Freemasons. Visitors can follow a particular timeline, or choose a random but equally compelling reading of London by cross-referencing the different word streams.

Together this *bricolage* of physical elements – of space, light, art and architecture – melds to create a particular sense of place. 'All things that can give ordinary life a turn for the better', said the water-sculptor William Pye, 'are useless. Affection, laughter, poetry, art and all. But they are not valueless, and not ineffectual, either.'[1] Plantation Lane is offered as an antidote to universalised commercial public space, with its flotsam of randomly competing retail signage, advertising billboards, and street furniture. Instead, this is a pause – a breathing space, intended not so much to offer answers as to invite reflection from those who chance upon it.

Reference

1   William Pye, quoted by Jay Merrick in Paul Brislin (ed), *Plantation Lane: Time and Tide*, Wordsearch (London), 2005, p 13.

Above and left
Plantation Lane: contemporary context

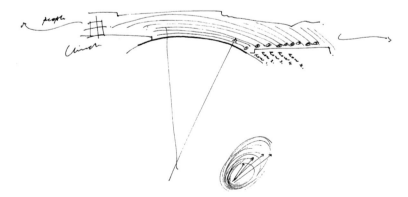

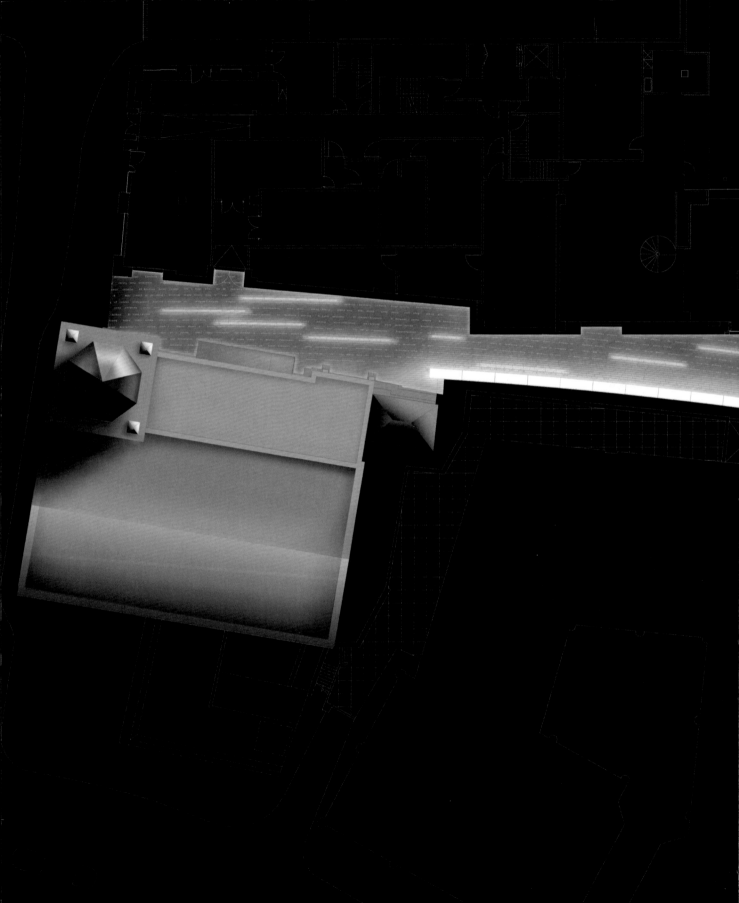

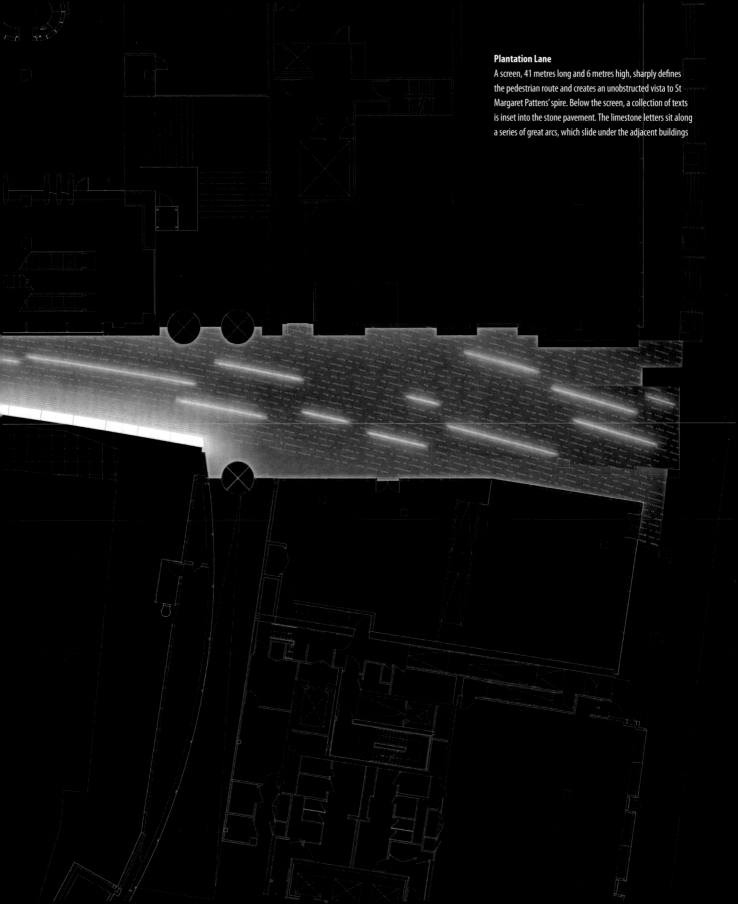

Plantation Lane

A screen, 41 metres long and 6 metres high, sharply defines the pedestrian route and creates an unobstructed vista to St Margaret Pattens' spire. Below the screen, a collection of texts is inset into the stone pavement. The limestone letters sit along a series of great arcs, which slide under the adjacent buildings

ROW 29:
[ ] y of London Underground Stations/etymology etc:
Aldgate/Aelgate
Aldgate East (see Aldgate)
Angel/Angel Inn
Arsenal/Arsenal Football Club
Bank/Bank of England
Barbican/Barbicana (Saxon: burgh kennin)
Bermondsey/Vermundesi c. 712
Bethnal Green/Blithedale
Blackfiars/Black Friars Monastery 13th century
Borough/Old English 'burh-a fortified place'
Cannon Street/Candelwichstrete c. 1180 (from
        Candle and Old English 'wic, a market')
Chancery Lane/Newstrate (New Street)
Farringdon/Farringdon Street
Holborn/Holebourne 951
Liverpool/Lord Liverpool 1829
Moorgate/Moor Gate 1451
St Paul's/St Paul's Cathedral
Temple/The Knights Templars
Tower Hill/Tourhulle 1343
Limehouse/Le Lymhostes 1367+++

ROW 32:
[ ] Martin's le Grand c. 1056 (collegiate church of)
c) Holy Trinity Priory Aldgate (Augustinian) 1108
d) St Bartholomew's Hospital 1123
e) St Bartholomew's Priory (Augustinian) 1123
f) Hospital of St Mary 1197
g) St Helen's Priory (Benedictine) c. 1200-15
h) Greyfriars (Franciscan) 1225
j) Hospital of St Thomas of Acon 1227-8
k) Hospital of St Anthony 1243
l) Priory of St Mary Bethelehem
[ ]   (Bedlam Hospital) 1247
m) Austin Friars 1253
n) Blackfriars (Dominican) 1275
o) Holy Trinity Abbey, Minories
        (Order of St Clare) 1298
p) Crutched Friars (Order of the Holy Cross) 1298
q) Elsing Spital 1331

ROW 35:
[ ] oman Invasion
60 Boudicca burns London
120 A Great Fire
125-30 Hadrianic Fire
457 Saxons sack London
851 London attacked by Vikings
959 A Great Fire: St Paul's burned
994 London besieged by Danes
Invasions and Disasters:
1016 Third Danish siege
1066 Norman Conquest
1290 Expulsion of the Jews
1348 The Black Death
1406 The Plague
1665 The Great Plague
1666 The Great Fire
1940 The beginning of The Blitz
1987 Black Mon[ ]

ROW 38:
[ ] idge
Chiswick Bridge
Barnes Bridge
Hammersmith Bridge
Putney Bridge
Wandsworth Bridge
Battersea Bridge
Albert Bridge
Chelsea Bridge
Vauxhall Bridge
Lambeth Bridge
Westminster Bridge
Thames Crossings:
Hungerford Foot Bridge
Waterloo Bridge
Blackfriars Bridge
Millennium Bridge
Southwark Bridge
London Bridge
Tower Bridge
Rotherhithe Tunnel
Greenwich Foot Tunnel
Blackwall Tunnel

ROW 41:
+++ Wormwood Street
Camomile Street
Vine Street
Grape Street
Mulberry Gardens
Ivy Lane
Grass Church Street
Rosemary Lane
Saffron Hill
[ ] Primrose Street
Dirty Alley
Dirty Hill
Dirty Lane
Addle Street
Foul Lane
Deadman's Place
Gutter Lane
Dunghill
Midden Lane
Laystall Street
Shiteburn Lane
Stinking Alley
St Ercenwald Street
Costermonger Row
Limeburner Lane

ROW 44:
[ ] ater noster Row
Ave Maria Lane
Creed Court
Amen Court
Pilgrim Street
Trinity Place
Pope's Head Alley
Jerusalem Passage
Idol Lane
Pardon Churchyard
Wilderness Row
Carmelite Street
Whitefriars Street
Blackfriars Broadway
Mitre Street
Crutched Friars
The Minories
Worship Street

ROW 47:
[ ] ch
Covent Garden
Plough Court
Markets and gardens:
Long Acre
Moorfields
Partridge Alley
Swan Alley
Haymarket
Park Lane
Hog Lane
Spitalfields
Smithfields
Lincoln's Inn Fields
Springs-Wells:
Holywell Street
Sadler's Wells
Clerkenwell
Spa Fields
Monkwell Square

ROW 50:
[ ] es for London:
Londuniu
Lundenwic
Londinium
Longidinium
Lundunaborg
Cockaigne
Laindon
Llyn-don
Trinovantum
Caer Ludd
Lundunes
Lundene
Lundone
Lindonion
Ludenberk
The Big Smoke
The Great Wen
Other London Rivers:
The Stand
Queenhithe
Rotherhithe
Lea

ROW 53:
+ the Sun, Prince Adept 28°
Knight of Saint Andrew 29°
Grand Elected Knight Kadosh, Knight of the
    Black & White Eagle 30°
33° of Freemasonry:
Grand Inspector Inquisitor Commander 31°
Sublime Prince of the Royal, Secret 32°
Sovereign Grand Inspector General 33°+++

ROW 56:
+++ Seventy King's Heads
Ninety King's Arms
Fifty Queen's Heads
Seventy Crowns
Fifty Roses
Twenty-five Royal Oaks
Thirty Bricklayers Arms
Fifteen Waterman's Arms
Sixteen Black Bulls
Twenty Cocks
Thirty Foxes
Thirty Swans+++

ROW 59:
+++ Bartholomew's Fair Mayfair
Cloth Fair
Southwark Fair
Clare Market
Stocks Market Cheapside
Fairs/Markets:
Coldbath Fields
Rag Fair
Smithfields Market
Penny Fields
Billingsgate
Borough Market
Fleet Market
Petticoat Lane
Field Lane
Leadenhall

ROW 62:
[ ] nd Hidden Rivers West to East:
Stamford Brook
The Wandle
Counter's Creek
The Falcoln
The Westbourne
The Tyburn
The Effra
Fleet
Walbrook
Neckinger
The Earl's Sluice
The Peck
The Ravensbourne

ROW 65:
+++ Sporting Streets:
Knightrider Street
Bear Street
Love Lane
Maid Lane
Addle Street
Cock Lane
Gropecontelane
Giltspur Street
Sweetings Alley
Shaft Alley
Bowling Green Lane+++

ROW 68:
[ ] te Hill
Ludgate Hill
London Hills:
Tothill
Parliament Hill
Tower Hill (White Mound)
Penton Hill/Pentonville
St Hermit's Hill
Cornhill
Snowhill
Dowgate Hill
Peter's Hill

ROW 71:
+++ Plagues:
The Black Death 1348
Plague 1406
The Sweating Sickness 1484
The Great Plague 1665
The Great Stink 1858
Typhus 1905
The Great Smog 1952+++

ROW 74:
[ ] atergate
Newgate
Aldersgate
Ludgate
Moorgate
Cripplegate
Bishopsgate
Aldgate
Albiongate
Billingsgate
St John's Gate
Broadgate

ROW 77:
Glory
Wisdom
Thanksgiving
Honour
Power
Bells of St Stephen, Rochester Row:
Might
Be Unto Our God For Ever And Ever Amen
Alleluiah

ROW 80:
+ Bethlehem/Bedlam
Prisons/Madhouses:
Marshalsea
Clink
Newgate
St Mary's Barking

ROW 83:
+ Moll Cut-Purse
Criminals:
Jack Sheppard+

ROW 86:
Mithras
Odin
Gog
Magog
Isis
Hermes+

ROW 89:
[ ] uddledock
Bell Wharf Lane
Cardinal's Wharf

ROW 92:
[ ] ditch
Cattestreet
Houndsditch

ROW 95:
+ Gundulf (?1024-1108)+

ROW 98:
[ ] dward III

[ ] Indicates text hidden beneath building.
+ Indicates spacing instructions to stone mason.
    Each cross represents a 125mm module.

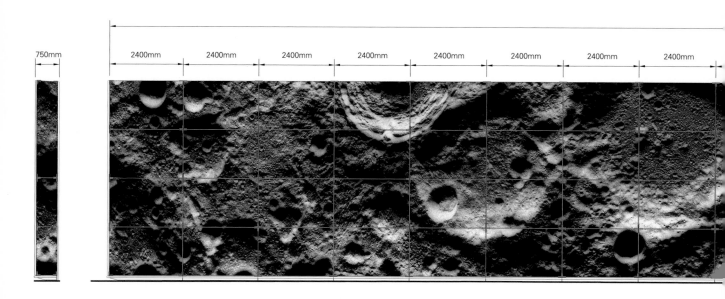

750mm   2400mm   2400mm   2400mm   2400mm   2400mm   2400mm   2400mm   2400mm

750mm

Plan

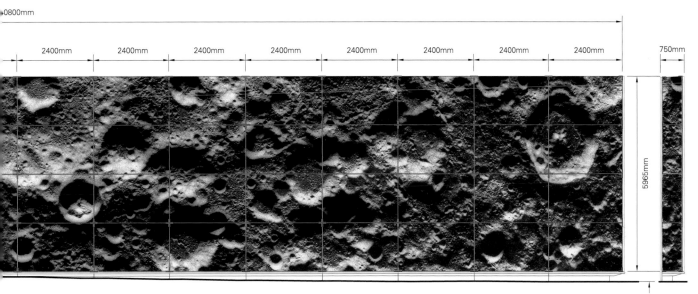

0800mm

| 2400mm | 2400mm | 2400mm | 2400mm | 2400mm | 2400mm | 2400mm | 2400mm | 750mm |

5965mm

Farside Terra, Moon

Enlarged detail of re-mastered photograph of the highlands on
the dark side of the moon, originally taken from a distance of 1600
kilometres by the Apollo 16 astronaut Kenneth Mattingly, in April
1972. The image was reproduced by Simon Patterson from the book
Full Moon by Michael Light

Elevation

41

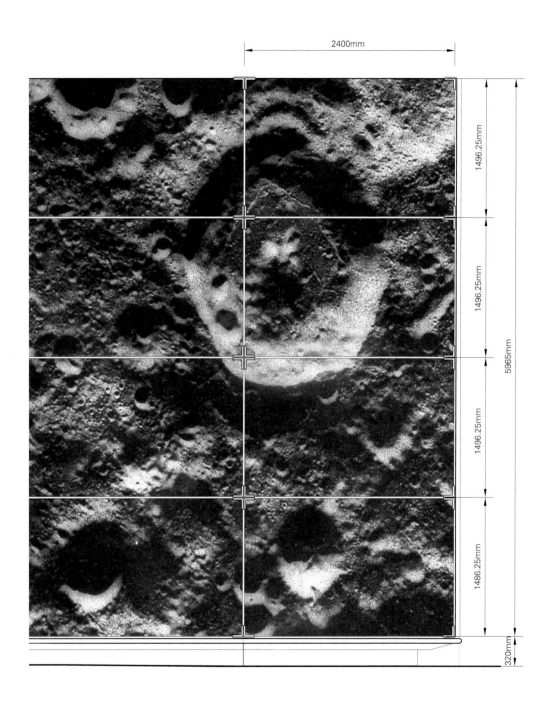

2400mm

1496.25mm

1496.25mm

5965mm

1496.25mm

1486.25mm

320mm

Elevation

750mm

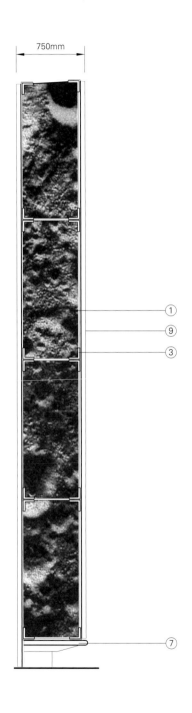

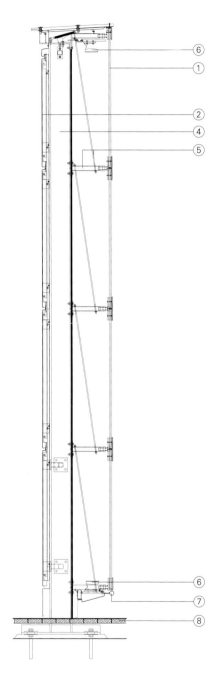

① Glass
② Hook-on aluminium panel
③ Stainless-steel fixing bracket
④ Structural-steel column
⑤ Steel support tube & tie rod
⑥ LED light fitting
⑦ Stainless-steel bull bar
⑧ Stone floor
⑨ Stainless-steel edge frame

Elevation

Section

Left and below

Light screen interior and exterior: cyan colour phase

Above
Light screen: interior colour progression

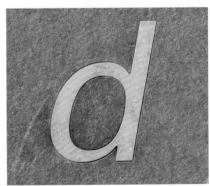

Right
Jura limestone letter set into Pietra del Cardoso floor slab

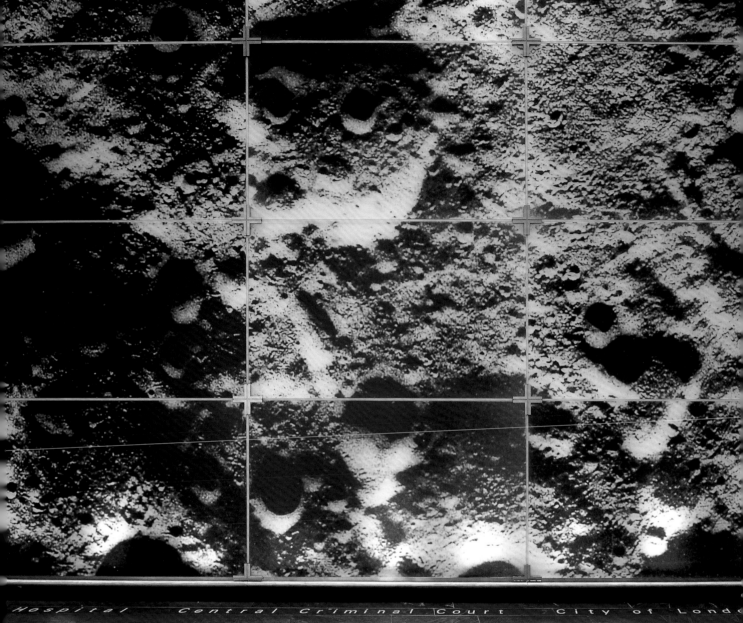

Hospital   Central Criminal Court   City of Londo

rocers   3) Drapers   4) Fishmongers   5) Go

t Sepulchre   St Martin Ludgate   St And

t Magnus the Martyr   St Dunstan-in-

Magnus Clemens Maximus (d. 388

ht of the East & West 17°

Victoria/victory   Vult

Left and following pages
Time lapse sequence

Right
Folding entry gates, closed only once a year
to maintain right of ownership

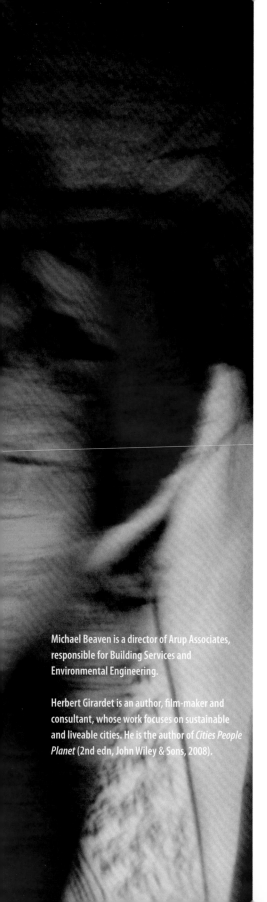

Michael Beaven is a director of Arup Associates, responsible for Building Services and Environmental Engineering.

Herbert Girardet is an author, film-maker and consultant, whose work focuses on sustainable and liveable cities. He is the author of *Cities People Planet* (2nd edn, John Wiley & Sons, 2008).

Sustaining Design

Herbert Girardet in conversation with Michael Beaven:

Arup Associates' quest for whole life sustainability

Another world is not only possible, she is on her way.
On a quiet day, I can hear her breathing.

Arundhati Roy, Porto Alegre, 2003[1]

The challenges of modern building design are staggering. Compared with the structures of the past, buildings are highly complicated – not only because of the availability of many new construction materials, but also because their uses are fundamentally different. Today, above all, buildings are containers for a vast array of electrical appliances that require complex infrastructures in their own right. Meanwhile humans – who sometimes seem to figure merely as add-on extras, there only to service the electronics – have the audacity to want comfortable spaces in which to live and work, too!

The problem is compounded by the growing distance between architects and developers as globalisation makes the ownership arrangements of buildings increasingly anonymous. Then along come legislators, pestered by NGOs, to complicate matters even further. They demand significant improvements to the environmental performance of buildings, which are major contributors to ecological deterioration and climate change. Building design is thus increasingly governed by legislation that aims at last to reduce the global consequence of local emissions.

Buckminster Fuller makes a highly pertinent point: 'You never change things by fighting the existing reality. To change something, build a new model that makes the existing model obsolete.'[2] Arup Associates' concept of unified design is just such a new model – a powerful tool to ensure that resources are used responsibly, and that development is sustainable.

The need for this approach is evident when we look at the global impact of major cities, which will soon be the primary human habitat. These sophisticated complexes are not only the largest structures we have made – they have a voracious appetite. Modern cities greedily use up the bulk of the world's natural and manmade products. Sited on just 3 to 4 per cent

Right
Buildings are responsible for up to half of a
city's total energy consumption

of the world's land surface, they contain half of the earth's population and consume 75 to 80 per cent of her resources. Of these, fossil fuels are the worst environmental pollutants. A huge demand for energy defines modern cities. Vast agglomerations with tens of millions of inhabitants were impossible before the age of coal, oil, gas, steel, industrial mass production and global trade. These great organisms depend on a continuous supply of energy – to operate their internal and external transportation systems; to erect steel, concrete and glass structures that could not function without air conditioning, and without lifts ceaselessly going up and down.

The role that buildings play is dramatic: they are responsible for up to half a city's total energy consumption. The energy use and carbon dioxide emission of sophisticated offices are high, but even this scenario is eclipsed by the world's data centres. These now generate the same volume of carbon emissions as the average European country, and more than double those of Finland and Portugal.[3]

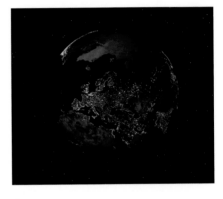

Above
Energy demand, perceived from space. London, Paris and the
Rhur are clearly visible, while North America lights the horizon

Mike Beaven, a director at Arup Associates, has strong views on the way forward: 'Sustainability brings people together around a common theme. This is a critical time for society and its relationship with the planet's eco-systems. The moment is right for radical thinking. Unified design is the mechanism by which to get to the next step: to understand how we can minimise human impact and maximise human opportunity.'

Arup Associates has always practised integrated design, a process whereby architects, structural engineers and building services engineers develop projects collaboratively in a single studio. Unified design is deliberately both deeper and wider than this, also involving environmentalists, psychologists, human behaviour specialists and other experts. It focuses on people from the outset. The greater spectrum of professional expertise offers a much broader horizon of opportunity. Apart from helping designers and clients think differently, Arup Associates has found that this expansive process of collaboration also maximises innovation: the creative output is far greater than the sum of its parts; and the results are often unexpected.

Unified design's radical pandisciplinary approach is infused by a sustainable development philosophy. An appropriate response to the energy economy underpins all decision making – a legacy of four decades of low-energy design at Arup Associates. But more than this, the practice believes that designs must achieve a whole life sustainability.

Learning from Ladakh

We can see the earliest precursors of a unified design strategy in operation in a modest
project in Ladakh, Northern India. The approach to this project reaches beyond obvious
notions of energy saving; it seeks to maintain indigenous culture and tradition too, through
a focus on the importance of human experience, the senses and memory. Whole life
sustainability searches for ways to enhance the existing value systems found within different
locations, rather than to create Modernist models that expect people, cities and places
around the world to behave in identical ways.

Designers Arup Associates, together with engineers from the wider Arup group, have been
engaged with the Druk White Lotus School since 1997. It's been a journey along a learning
curve between architects, engineers, constructors and the school itself. Generations of
designers have led the project, and many others have benefited from their involvement.

Here, the challenge is to create a centre of local culture, education and communication that
integrates Ladakh's unique cultural and architectural heritage – so well adapted to extreme
climatic conditions – with the opportunities inherent in contemporary eco-design. The
project seeks to minimise its own environmental impact, but also aims to help the local
community thrive. In other parts of India, long-established values are being eroded by
modernisation and younger generations are attracted away from this remote area. Against
this backdrop the school attempts to nurture a self-sustaining traditional culture that
redresses the imbalance.

The local community and the designers have shared their expertise to produce a building
that is deeply embedded in the Ladakhi way of life. It does this through a range of
sustainability features that can be defined in both cultural and ecological terms. The resulting
buildings are a fascinating reflection of an inter-cultural dialogue.

According to Mike Beaven the project is dynamic: it embraces a wide variety of enthusiastic
designers and a client driven to create a project in a different way. 'Working with the Trust
was an immensely powerful learning experience for the practice, which brought important
innovations including the use of trombe wall and thermal-mass techniques in a low-tech
environment to capture and preserve solar heat for the residences. Arup Associates' designers
contributed their expertise in harnessing natural energy, light and sunlight, and their
experience of passive design and earthquake resistant buildings. In turn, they also learned
much about combining modern ecological design with vernacular construction. The roof
construction, for example, was adapted from a regional tradition completely suited to the

Below
The masterplan of the Druk White Lotus School is inspired by the
Mandala: practical functions are united with this metaphorical
representation of the universe

climate.' Wherever the Ladakhi methods were more suitable the team adopted them and changed the design accordingly, or allowed the design to evolve with the community craftsmen. While it is sometimes challenging to engage users with these technologies, in this case the outcome rewarded everyone.

In this cultural interchange, building design and educational content are linked. Engineers and architects gain invaluable local experience, which is returned to London. On the other hand, Arup Associates learned that vigorous interaction with the school's users is also essential to make the design work: to communicate a clear understanding of the specific features of the building; for instance, how the trombe wall ventilation screens should be opened at certain times and closed at others to ensure a pleasant internal environment; or the recycling process of the dry, naturally ventilated pit latrines. The industry as a whole still has much to learn about this culturally sensitive, powerfully interactive approach.

Another forward-thinking aspect of the East–West dialogue involves new ecological investment models. Arup Associates is using the school in its carbon emission offset strategy, to mutual advantage. In 2008, the Drukpa Trust will see investment from Arup Associates' carbon offset fund provide photovoltaic panels for the school that will supply solar energy to power computers, lights and laboratory equipment. All benefit from this relationship. Arup Associates' carbon is balanced; they know precisely how their investment is being used; and the school will run a diesel generator far less often within its grounds. The symbiotic relationship that has evolved through this unassuming project is an important model for the stimulation of sustainable development in fragile ecological environments.

The Sky is the Limit

A unified design methodology has been employed by Arup Associates to create the new Sky centre on the western periphery of London. Harlequin 1 will house recording, post-production and transmission facilities for Sky's Broadcast and Sports News departments, including naturally ventilated studios and office space and free-cooled data rooms for more than 400 computer servers. This is a large building, roughly equivalent in scale to two New York city blocks.

Broadcasting facilities are substantial users of energy, but Arup Associates was supported by an enthusiastic client. Sky desired a building that could deal with its significant complexities in a truly sustainable manner: an exemplar of environmental and energy efficiency that featured strong engagement with the business and surrounding community.

Below
The masterplan of the Druk White Lotus School is inspired by the
Mandala: practical functions are united with this metaphorical
representation of the universe

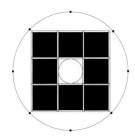

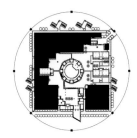

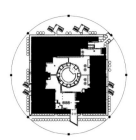

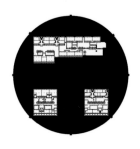

Above
Druk White Lotus School: construction methods adapted
from Ladakhi tradition

User response was embraced as a central component of the unified design strategy. In the Sky building each of the multiple design options was exhaustively tested by a very large – and extremely demanding – specialist group. The net result was significant. Harlequin 1 is the most sustainable broadcasting, studio and data-centre building of its genre yet designed. It also contains the world's first naturally ventilated recording studios – a perfect solution to a design challenge not even anticipated at the outset.

The studios are of particular interest, a technological *tour de force*. They require very close control of external noise and so natural ventilation would appear to be counter-intuitive, as noise is normally brought in along with the fresh air. In response Arup Associates have designed a system driven by the waste heat given off by the studio lights. Hot air from the lights would usually need to be cooled mechanically. In this case the air is allowed to rise out through giant ventilation chimneys visible on the exterior of the building, drawing in cool, fresh, external air below the studios through a series of sound attenuators. Where external conditions are inappropriate for natural ventilation, mechanical ventilation and cooling of the studio spaces can be implemented.

Unified design's extensive collaborative approach provided the basis for the studio ventilation: a solution that arose from an extremely close working relationship between Arup Acoustics; the mechanical, structural, electrical engineers and architects of Arup Associates; and expert client and industry specialists.

Sky's brief for a genuinely sustainable headquarters challenged Arup Associates radically to minimise energy use throughout, and to capture every viable natural resource close to the site. Intriguingly, Sky's ultimate aim is to go beyond zero carbon emission by means of the construction of a highly energy efficient building powered by a locally sourced, biomass-fuelled Combined Cooling, Heating and Power (CCHP) plant. This is planned not only to serve Sky, but also other buildings around the site. The CCHP will provide enough renewable energy to reduce the carbon emissions from Harlequin 1 by at least 20 per cent. Moreover, sufficient flexibility has been built into the infrastructure to ensure that future new sustainable technologies such as, for example, hydrogen fuel cells, can be incorporated into the project.

Within the project, 100 per cent of the structural timber will be from sustainable sources; a substantial percentage of construction materials are from local sources; and a minimum 50 per cent of the construction, demolition and land clearing waste will be recycled or salvaged. Already, 90 per cent of the demolished building material on the Harlequin 1 site have been

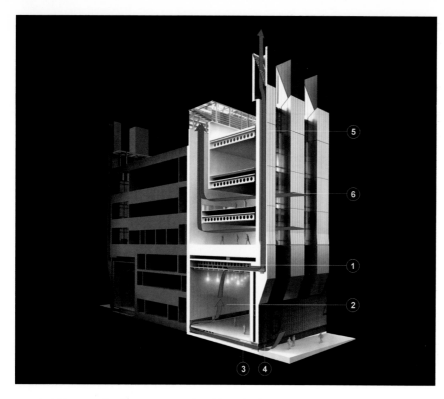

1 Waste heat from the studio lights and equipment rises through the studio ventilation chimneys. The chimney tops harness external wind pressure to assist extraction
2 As waste heat rises, a small negative pressure is set up in the studios
3 This pressure drop overcomes the resistance of the sound attenuators, drawing in fresh cool air from the exterior
4 Exterior intake grilles
5 When external conditions are inappropriate for natural ventilation, mechanical ventilation and cooling of the studio spaces can be implemented using the same chimneys
6 Office natural ventilation chimney follows similar principles

Left

Natural ventilation strategies for studios and offices at Arup Associates' Sky Recording and Transmission Centre, London, 2010

recycled. Water use has been minimised and harvested rainwater will replace the potable water typically used to flush WCs throughout buildings.

Arup Associates' interest in whole life sustainability demands a focus a on the human experience of a building, too. The first stage of project design generated only a highly space efficient box. What was missing was the power of people to control their working environment: to 'own' it. To let the building breathe, the designers added circulation spaces and ventilation shafts that activated the place for people: spaces that are naturally ventilated and allow maximum daylight penetration wherever possible. A building management system optimises cooling and ventilation, monitoring weather conditions but, most important of all, control of the natural ventilation systems is handed back to every individual who works in the building.

Mike Beaven notes that this kind of project is usually massively energy consuming. He explains that what Arup Associates have done is to integrate a raft of processes and technologies that drastically reduce the energy profile of the building while ensuring that the way the building works is also sustainable from a human perspective. This unique project sets a worldwide benchmark for sustainability while demonstrating the benefits of a unified design approach.

Right
Naturally lit and ventilated spaces for people are woven into the highly technical Sky Recording and Transmission Centre

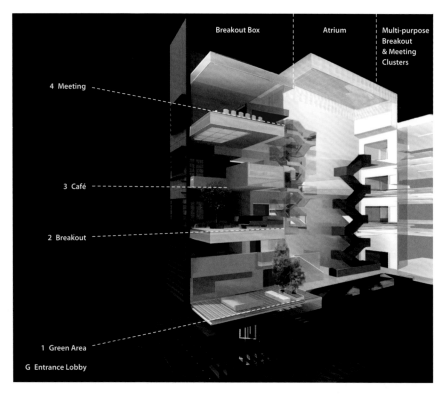

Of Server Farms and Data Centres

Buildings used for international communications are major users of energy and none more so than the data centres and server farms that make the large-scale storage and rapid transmission of data possible. These hubs power the global information transfers that drive the World Wide Web. Any architectural or engineering practice that is serious about engaging with difficult issues should focus on those areas that really affect the planet. Targeting data centres makes a difference.

There is much to be done to improve the energy performance of data centre operations. According to Fujitsu Siemens Computers, Britain's data centres – which hold some 880,000 servers – are generating an unnecessary 1.2 million tons of CO_2 a year. Why? Because they are poorly configured, with under-utilised servers and over-stressed air conditioning systems. Their emissions amount to more than the total annual CO_2 emissions of cities such as Norwich (942,000 tons) and Oxford (981,000 tons).[4]

One major operator, Google, maintains some 450,000 servers that are located in clusters across North America, in California, Virginia, Georgia, and Oregon; and also in EU countries such as Ireland and Belgium. The servers use vast amounts of electricity. Meanwhile, progressive server companies are becoming increasingly environmentally conscious and are starting to set up facilities in places that are favourable to the production of renewable electricity – sunlit desert locations with predominantly blue skies.[5] In 2009 Google plans to build a server centre in Iowa on a site with abundant wind power resources. This has a twofold rationale: the location allows the company to fulfil its strong green energy objectives; and it is close to fibre-optic communications links.[6]

Major energy consuming structures require a twin approach: the use of renewable energy to power data and server centres; and the more efficient use of that energy. In this context, Arup Associates has been working with financial group Citi on the design of a major new data centre in Frankfurt. Citi wanted the most sustainable data centre possible. The holistic, broad-ranging unified design strategy drove new thinking. Commenting on the project, Mike Beaven notes that the company had used a combined approach: 'Through collaboration with the technical infrastructure team energy consumption was reduced by 25 per cent, using highly efficient and resilient systems, free cooling with water-based heat rejection and 100 per cent heat recovery. Despite a -10°C external temperature, there are no boilers'.

'In this project, we found that very efficient standby systems were essential. If batteries are employed to achieve the standby power requirement, there is a 5 per cent loss of power into the computers and essential systems all the time. But if diesel-rotary standby systems are installed, which use fly-wheels to store energy, then the losses are a fraction of a per cent. Since these rotary systems are also highly robust it is not surprising that they are incorporated in military defence systems. Arup Associates had to fight for these technologies, but eventually convinced Citi in the US, where batteries are the norm'.

The team also looked at other issues such as water efficiency. A reverse-osmosis system was installed to capture water, so reducing the chemical dosing by 95 per cent. A green roof covers almost the entire upper surface of the building, and the landscape is 'zero-watering'.

The project demonstrates that it is possible significantly to reduce the environmental impact of data centres. The Citi scheme won the Green Data Centre of the Year award, and it is set to achieve LEED Gold – and possibly Platinum – standard, amazing many architects who had written off data centres as simply 'wasteful'. Even a small reduction in the carbon output of immense energy consumers is important, while significant reductions are clearly of massive benefit to mankind.

Sustainable Cities

To create sustainable buildings, as well as cities, we would be well advised to develop a clear understanding of how natural systems work and how manmade structures could be designed – or redesigned – to function as sustainable systems that are compatible with the natural world. Nature's own ecosystems have an essentially circular metabolism. Nature knows no waste: every output by an ecosystem contributes to the continuous renewal of the whole living environment of which it is a part. The web of life hangs together in a chain of mutual benefit. To become sustainable, cities and individual buildings have to mimic nature's

Above
Chongming Island, the site of the zero-carbon Dongtan Eco-City, near Shanghai, designed by Arup and Arup Associates. An overarching sustainability framework balances development needs with ecological objectives. The first phase of completion is due in 2010 with 10,000 inhabitants

circular systems, using and re-using resources efficiently and eliminating waste discharges that are not compatible with the natural world.

Crucially, the future of civilisation depends on utilising the rich knowledge of all people: a central concept of unified design. If we decide to develop sustainable structures and processes, we need to create a cultural context in which this can occur. In the end, only a wide-ranging change in attitudes – perhaps even a profound spiritual and ethical shift – can bring about the deeper transformations required.

It is evident that we can mastermind a revolution in urban problem solving that benefits city dwellers as much as it reduces their impact on the globe. A wide variety of new approaches to urban planning and resource management is now available to us. To implement them we need vigorous new partnerships between all stakeholders – national governments, local authorities, community groups, NGOs and the private sector.

At the urban scale, Arup and Arup Associates are seeding sustainable projects, as they become ever more actively involved not just in the design of individual buildings, but increasingly in urban masterplanning and ecological reconstruction work too. Stratford City in the UK and Dongtan Eco-City in China are the best known examples. Here, a unified design approach will almost certainly prove to be highly effective.

Mike Beaven recalls Arup Associates' first meetings with the Dongtan client and how the practice started thinking about an overarching sustainability framework, as the client struggled to assimilate the information contained in hundreds of separate studies, with no mechanism to understand the whole. In response, Arup Associates proposed a framework that brought together diverse interests and developed perspective; it gave the client the keys to release the land value in a sensitive piece of the environment while maintaining the ecological objective of preserving the bird life habitat on the adjacent mud flats. 'The world's cities require much more comprehensive and compelling propositions like this: with aspirational standards, reached through consultation with the affected communities. The methodology must require "thinking bigger" – and that supplier and client think and act together.'

Fortunately for our futures, this kind of unified approach is becoming much more common. The power of legal planning frameworks must be harnessed to give these ideas 'teeth'. The structures we create have great longevity, and frameworks help maintain the initial vision; to retain it over years and years of development. The timescale of a designer's involvement can't just be 'in and out': it has to be part of the fabric that is left behind. In cities all over the world a significant start has been made – now let us realise the full potential of these opportunities.

Shaping the Future

Winston Churchill noted that 'we shape our buildings, and thereafter they shape us.'[7] It is crucial to learn lessons from designs that have gone wrong, particularly the experiences of the architecture of the 1960s and '70s. The disposable buildings that characterise this period have left a sad legacy of disposability that is ingrained in contemporary culture. This era of cheap energy was also one of cheap buildings, of buildings that lacked the subtlety and complexity which are the goal of the human mind at its best. It is time to accept that mistakes were made. Unified design is an approach that allows us to get things right by relying on a multilayered network of influences to shape the final building and the urban landscape beyond. Efficient energy and resource use must now be united with a clear understanding of how people can enjoy the structures in which they live and work. Unified design has the makings of a methodology that is fit for the stringent requirements of the 21st century in which, at long last, we have started to appreciate that sustainability and resilience are the keys to the future.

As Ove Arup said in 1980, anticipating the concept of unified design: 'When engineers and quantity surveyors discuss aesthetics and architects study what cranes do, we are on the right road.'[8] Ove was correct in his vision of a society in which boundaries must be blurred and roles reversed if we are to create a better future. But perhaps it is even more fitting to adapt the words of Churchill: if we are to have any impact on the future at all, we must shape our minds to shape the buildings that will shape us hereafter.

This essay was developed in a series of conversations between Herbert Girardet and Michael Beaven during December 2007

References

1   From Arundhati Roy's speech, 'Confronting Empire' given at the World Social Forum
    at Porto Alegre, Brazil, 27 January 2003.

2   Buckminster Fuller cited in the Buckminster Fuller Institute Newsletter, vol 8 No. 3,
    http://www.bfi.org/ds_news_v8_n3

3   www.computing.co.uk/computing/news/2201365/centres-hike-co2-levels-3570869

4   www.smartplanet.com/news/business/10000320/data-centres-emit-more-co2-than-norwich-
    says-fujitsu-siemens-computers.htm

5   http://money.cnn.com/2007/10/03/technology/solar_servers.biz2/index.htm

6   http://en.wikipedia.org/wiki/Google_platform

7   Winston Churchill, *Time* magazine, 12 September 1960.

8   Widely attributed to Ove Arup and cited in http://www.bristol.ac.uk/civilengineering/aboutus/
    engineeringquotes.html. Peter Jones, author of *Ove Arup, Masterbuilder of the Twentieth Century*,
    Yale University Press (New Haven), notes that Ove used this comment frequently, from as early as
    the 1930s (Conversation with Arup Associates, 28 February 2008).

Vauxhall Transport Interchange, London

Arup Associates: Sustainable Regeneration

Vauxhall Transport Interchange
Sustainable Regeneration

The setting for this interchange would suit a modern-day Lear: the king's blasted heath replaced by the velocities and inertia of traffic, empty spaces and unremarkable existing buildings. Something momentous was required for this disjunctive urban site. Arup Associates' response is a sculptural ribbon of steel that undulates down the length of the Vauxhall bus station, delivering an entirely functional shelter and a sustainable device of landmark prominence.[1]

By day, the ribbon allows daylight to penetrate the entire circulation area and displays itself in the bold choice of material and articulation. By night it is an animated, floodlit beacon, offering visual excitement and a safe, well-lit environment. The elegant steel-clad flight-path brings a bold new elevational geometry to the area and a clarified signal of change.

But this is not gestural sculpture. The shelter is designed for people, and wrought entirely from their opinions. Won in public competition, this radical architectural presence was created after wide-ranging consultation at every design phase – a process central to the strategies of unified design. The key features are prompted by user desire. It was local demand that produced the *pissoirs* for homeward-bound clubbers, the open-sidedness, the clear sight lines, the extended CCTV coverage, and more retail points than originally mooted. Input also included response to choice of materials, fabric and colour.

Yet, at the same time, the Vauxhall building integrates sustainable principles as an inherent part of the design. The raking, cantilevered termination of the sheltering ribbon is more than a symbol of regeneration: it contains a series of state-of-the-art, high-efficiency photovoltaic cells, all oriented at precisely the right angle to the sky to maximise output. The cells combine ultra-thin amorphous silicon with monocrystalline technology to provide an optimum solution to London's cloudy skies.

Covering over 200 square metres of the upper surface of the long cantilevers, the photovoltaic cladding offers 27 megawatt hours of annual carbon free electricity, so delivering a significant proportion of the bus station's power requirements.[2] Below, a digitised read-out displays energy usage and carbon offset to passing travellers. Above, the prominence of the cantilevers renders the photovoltaic cells visible from the adjacent streets – both an important public demonstration of sustainable energy use, and an essential component of the Mayor of London's strategy for the use of renewable energy in public buildings.

The gritty surrounding area was previously notorious for its domination by traffic; its blighted pedestrian access. Through people oriented design, the interchange has become a community focal point – a safe urban environment that has stimulated local business and spurred the upgrade of other transport facilities in the area. This is now the second busiest interchange in the city. Bus usage has increased by 40 per cent, due in no small part to the extraordinarily wide consultation that underpinned the design process.

At Vauxhall Cross, unified design generates a striking ribbon of steel that is neither an empty icon nor a wilful gesture. Instead, we believe, this shelter is a completely functional symbol of integrated sustainability and urban renewal in London. But, most important of all, it is a space that people enjoy using.

Reference

1   Jay Merrick, 'Arup Associates Practice Profile', *Interior Atmospheres, Architectural Design*, May/June 2008, No 3, vol 78, pp 106-11.

2   Refer to p 156 for further information on the photovoltaic cladding.

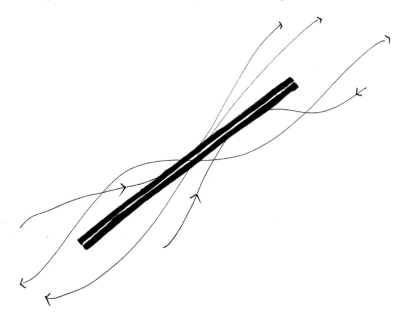

Previous pages
The dynamic rake of the cantilevers is oriented to generate the maximum possible output from the photovoltaic cells lining their upper surface

Below and following page
Animated sequence through the shelter: the sinuous canopy reflects the ephemeral movement of the transitory vehicles; while the dipping undulations provide places of enclosure and refuge. Above the canopy, photovoltaic cells are clearly visible

Left and previous page
Robust, transparent, human-scaled enclosures enhance a sense of
security and provide sheltered places for people

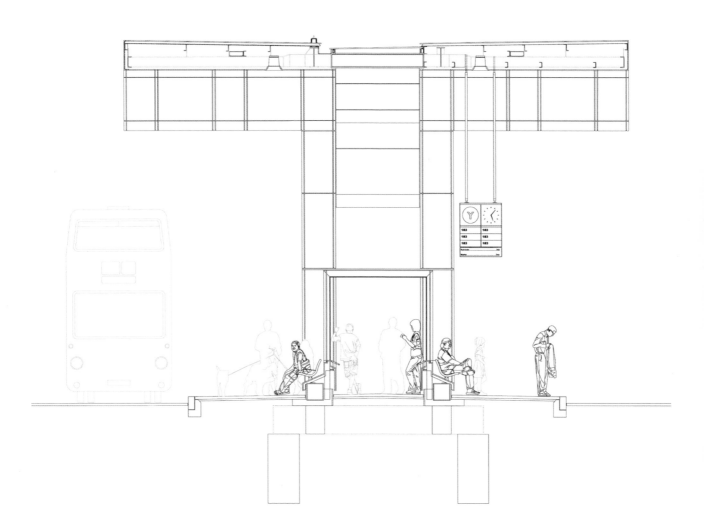

Above
Typical section through shelter

Above
The London Underground symbol is illuminated with colour
only at night. During the day it is transparent

Below and following page
The interchange is restless – a place of transience; and
yet within the undulating silver ribbon are places shaped
for human moments of stillness and reflection

Below and right
Sunlit shelter: even though robust and vandal resistant, the structure's design creates impromptu places for people to dwell

Part Two places the vision of people-focused design in the context of critical social thought outside of Arup Associates. **Juhani Pallasmaa** addresses the significance of the senses in design – particularly touch and sound, which have historically been repressed. **Leon van Schaik** discusses the importance of eidetic memory in design, highlighting the need for designers to look beyond traditional logical processes. A visual essay on **The Druk White Lotus School** demonstrates exemplary environmental and cultural sustainability in the Himalayas, through an architecture that engages the senses, memory and identity.

Reference
1   Jorge Luis Borges, *Selected Poems 1923-1967*, Penguin Books (London), 1985, in
     Juhani Pallasmaa, *The Eyes of the Skin*, John Wiley & Sons (Chichester), 2005, p 14.

TWO

THE WORLD OF THE SENSES

'…The taste of the apple…lies in the contact of the fruit with the palate, not in the fruit itself. In a similar way…poetry lies in the meeting of a poem and the reader, not in the lines of symbols printed on the pages of a book. What is essential is… the thrill of the almost physical emotion that comes with each reading.' [1]

Jorge Louis Borges

We can only relate to the material world through our senses. Our engagement with architecture is the same – empty of meaning without the interaction of people. Architecture needs to rediscover its potential to stimulate all the senses.

Architecture is unique among the arts – it carries a greater burden. Unlike other arts, where engagement is by choice, architecture is omnipresent. No other art form has the ability directly to enhance the quality of people's lives. Equally, no other art has the capacity to inflict as much misery. Our modes of creation must be cognisant of this responsibility, because our built environment is inextricably linked to our sense of self. If architecture is to rediscover its relevance to human experience, architects must recognise their unique obligation to reflect the widely diverse physical, cultural and emotional context in which their work is placed. Herein lies the unique power of architecture.

Unifying the Senses: Architecture as Lived Experience

Juhani Pallasmaa

Neglect and Exploitation of the Senses

Architecture has traditionally been theorised, taught and practised as an artform purely of the eye. As the functional, technical and economic factors of buildings tend to lose their significance over time and with the changing conditions of everyday life, the importance of their visual characteristics is further heightened. Even in our digital age, buildings continue to be regarded as aestheticised objects and judged primarily on their visual qualities. In fact, the dominance of vision has probably never been stronger than in the current era of the technologically expanded eye and mass-produced visual imagery, the 'unending rainfall of images', as Italo Calvino appropriately describes the present condition.[1]

As a consequence of the undue emphasis on vision, isolated from the other sensory realms and from an integrating existential sense, buildings are in danger of losing their material presence, hapticity and tactile intimacy as they turn into objects of mere visual seduction. It is also evident that an uncritical application of digital technologies tends further to advance the dominance of retinal imagery and the consequent perception of cold distance and alienation.

Today's architecture often aspires to become an object of admiration and wonder instead of seeking to concretise and integrate the human sense of existence, to be 'an instrument to confront the cosmos', to quote Gaston Bachelard's demanding definition of the metaphysical task of the house.[2] Yet, in addition to ever expanding rational, practical and technical tasks, architecture continues to have its primary mental and existential function.

Juhani Pallasmaa is an architect and author, who has held key academic positions in Helsinki and the US. He is widely published on topics that include cultural philosophy, environmental psychology, and the theory of art and architecture. His writings include the influential and enduring work *The Eyes of the Skin: Architecture and the Senses* (2nd edn, John Wiley & Sons, 2005). He is an Honorary Fellow of the AIA, a member of the International Committee of Architectural Critics, and a Member of the International Academy of Architecture.

Below
A tactile and caressing architectural space: the entrance hall, living room and main stairs of Alvar Aalto's Villa Mairea, Noormarkku, Finland 1938-9

Consumer culture has a blatantly dualistic attitude towards the senses as well as towards our embodied existence. On the one hand, the fundamental fact that we exist in the world through the senses and the cognitive processes is neglected in our established view of the human condition, something that is directly reflected in educational philosophies as well as in daily life. On the other, we are increasingly manipulated and exploited through our senses. Current consumer capitalism has covertly developed shrewd strategies of 'multisensory marketing' and a 'new technocracy of sensuality' for the purposes of sensory seduction and product differentiation. This commercial manipulation of the senses aims at creating a state of 'hyperesthesia' in today's consumer.[3]

Artificial scents are added to all kinds of products and spaces, and muzak subliminally conditions the shopper's mood. There have even been court actions brought to confirm a brand's monopoly over the auditory and olfactory aspects of a commodity in the same way that visual trademarks are legally protected.[4] No doubt we have already entered the era of manipulated and branded sensations. Branded signature architecture, aimed at creating eye-catching, recognisable and memorable visual images, is another example of this new sensory exploitation, 'to colonize by canalizing the "mind space" of the consumer'.[5]

While hardly being aware of it, we are living in an age of aestheticisation. Everything is aestheticised today: architecture, consumer products, personality and behaviour, politics and, ultimately, even war. An aestheticised surface appeal has replaced the depth of essence and social significance. Similarly, the social idealism and empathy that gave Modernism its optimism and compassion have been replaced by formalist aesthetic rhetoric.

Back to the Senses

Since the 1980s, the long neglect of the human sensory and sensual essence as well as the disregard of the embodied processes in our existential experience and cognition, have given rise to a swiftly expanding literature on the senses and the various dimensions of human embodiment extended all the way to processes of thinking.[6] Also in architectural writing and education the body and the senses have gained increasing weight, a burgeoning critical appreciation that is exemplified by philosopher David Michael Levin's statement: 'I think it is appropriate to challenge the hegemony of vision – the ocularcentrism of our culture. And I think we need to examine very critically the character of vision that predominates today in our world. We urgently need a diagnosis of the psychosocial pathology of everyday seeing – and a critical understanding of ourselves as visionary beings.'[7]

Above
Timber provides nurture in a hostile terrain:
Arup Associates, Druk White Lotus School,
Ladakh, Northern India, 1997–

Above
The perspectival city is the distanced city of the eye.
'The city of memory is empty because for an imagination it is easier
to conjure architecture than human beings' (Joseph Brodsky).
The Ideal City attributed to the school of Piero della Francesca,
early 16th century

I believe that many critical aspects of architecture today can likewise be understood through an analysis of the epistemology of the senses, and through a critique of the ocular bias of our culture at large, and of architecture in particular. The sense of alienation, distance and unyielding hardness in today's buildings and cityscapes can be understood as a consequence of the neglect of the needs of the body and the senses, as an imbalance of the sensory system, and the disappearance of the existential dimension of architecture. Instead of being cultural and metaphysical manifestations, buildings are increasingly turned into aestheticised objects of utility and economic profit.

The art of the detached eye has certainly produced imposing and thought-provoking architectural structures, but it has not facilitated human rootedness in the world, 'man's homecoming', to use a beautiful notion of Aldo van Eyck, who aspired to root contemporary architecture in its anthropological, mental and lived ground.[8] It has to be emphasised, however, that regardless of these negative general tendencies, extraordinarily sensuous, rich and meaningful buildings are being conceived even today and that these projects constitute an important architectural resistance to the present erosion of human and cultural values.

Numerous writers have pointed out the biased dominance of the eye, 'the hegemony of vision', in the history of Western culture in general and especially in today's reality of mass-produced visual images. A characteristic of vision – in fact of all the senses – that has been studied much less is its implicit tendency to interact and integrate with the other sense modalities. The highly welcome interest in the significance of the senses has tended to regard these as independent and detached realms instead of understanding our sensory relation to the world as a fully integrated existential interaction. 'The hands want to see, the eyes want to caress', as Goethe perceptively observed.[9]

Hierarchy of the Senses

Since Aristotle, touch has been regarded as the lowest of the senses; it is to him that the entire notion of the five senses is usually attributed, and it is he who established the hierarchy, placing them in descending order: vision, hearing, smell, taste and touch.[10] Instead of viewing these five as independent and isolated the psychologist James J Gibson categorises them in five sensory systems: visual system, auditory system, the taste-smell

system, the basic-orienting system and the haptic system. Steinerian philosophy goes further, arguing that we actually use no less than twelve senses.[11]

In addition to being regarded as the noblest of the senses, vision has also been connected with thinking and the notion of truth, granting it added authority. Already classical Greek thought based certainty on vision and visibility: 'The eyes are more exact witnesses than the ears', wrote Heraclitus in one of his fragments.[12] Plato even sees the origins of philosophy in vision:

> [T]he supreme benefit for which sight is responsible is that not a word of all that we have said about the universe could have been said if we had not seen stars, and sun and heaven. As it is, the sight of day and night, the months and returning years, the equinoxes and solstices, has caused the invention of number, given us the notion of time, and made us inquire into the nature of the universe; thence we have derived philosophy, the greatest gift the gods have ever given or will give to mortals. This is what I call the greatest good our eyes give us.[13]

In addition to the visual bias of Western thought, almost all our knowledge of past cultures is recorded in the visual order; human history 'exists in matter and space rather than time and sound'.[14]

The comparatively lowly position of touch resulted from the observation that it was a capacity found in all animals. In Aristotle's view, touch is needed for being, whereas the other senses are necessary for *wellbeing*.[15] Medieval, Renaissance and Enlightenment thought continued to consider smell, taste and touch merely as the domain of beasts.[16] This strictly hierarchical and moralising view has prevailed to this day, as the three lower senses are seen as having only private functions. However, the relative roles of the senses are culturally determined and there are significant differences in how the various sense modalities are emphasised across cultures. In some cultures, for instance, our private senses have social functions. In Western understanding, the importance of the sense of touch is slowly emerging from the shadow of more than two millennia of biased thought. We are finally discovering that the lowest sense may well end up being the most important one.

Primacy of Touch

All the senses, including vision, are extensions of tactile experience; in fact, even Aristotle describes taste and seeing as forms of touching.[17] The senses are the result of specialisation of skin tissue, and all sensory experiences are modes of touching, and thus fundamentally related to tactility. Our contact with the world takes place at the boundary of the self; the senses are amazing extensions of the physical human body: 'Through vision we touch the sun and the stars'.[18]

Skin and the sense of touch are essential in Michel Serres"philosophy of mingled bodies':[19] 'In the skin, through the skin, the world and the body touch, defining their common border. Contingency means mutual touching: world and body meet and caress the skin. I do not like to speak of the place where my body exists as a milieu, preferring rather to say that things mingle… The skin intervenes in the things of the world and brings about their mingling.'[20] Even more importantly than rendering a boundary, touch is the sensory mode that integrates our experience of the world with our selves. Even visual perceptions are fused and integrated into the haptic continuum of the self; my body remembers who I am and how I am located in the world. The miraculous consistency of the world cannot possibly arise from fragmentary visual imagery; the world is held together by the haptic sense and our sense of self. My sensing and sensual body is truly the navel of my world, not as the view point of a central perspective, but as the sole focus of integration, reference, memory and imagination. 'I am what is around me,' argues Wallace Stevens;[21] 'I am the space where I am', establishes Noel Arnaud;[22] and, finally, 'I am my world', concludes Ludwig Wittgenstein.

The senses are not merely passive receptors of stimuli; they actively reach out, seek, investigate and shape the entity of the world and ourselves. The senses and our bodily being are centres of tacit knowledge and they structure our being-in-the-world. All our senses as well as our very being 'think' in that they grasp utterly complex existential situations. In fact, medieval philosophy identified the existence of a sixth unifying sense, that of selfhood, through which the self acknowledges itself as itself. Serres associates this capacity of self-awareness with the skin and the faculty of touch.[23]

Integration of the Senses

We do not only touch with vision, but we also induce, project and experience auditive, olfactory and gustatory qualities through visual means. Besides, all our perceptions are in constant but subconscious interaction with memories, dreams and imaginings. Altogether, the senses do not mediate specific and categorised percepts. They are integrated in the full experience of the world and the self, the very existential sense.

In his seminal book *Art as Experience,*[24] first published in 1934, John Dewey points out the significance of this sensory interplay and exchange:

> *Qualities of sense, those of touch and taste as well as of sight and hearing, have aesthetic quality. But they have it not in isolation but in their connections: as interacting, not as simple and separate entities. Nor are connections limited to their own kind, colors to colors, sounds with sounds… The eye, ear and whatever, is only the channel through which the total response takes place… In seeing a picture, it is not true that visual qualities are as such, or consciously, central, and other qualities arranged about them in an accessory or associated fashion. Nothing could be further from the truth… When we perceive, by means of the eyes as causal aids, the liquidity of water, the coldness of ice, the solidity of rocks, the bareness of trees in winter, it is certain that other qualities than those of the eye are conspicuous and controlling in perception. And it is as certain as anything can be that optical qualities do not stand out by themselves with tactual and emotive qualities clinging to their skirts… Any sensuous quality tends, because of its organic connections, to spread and fuse.*[25]

The philosopher is not referring here to the somewhat exceptional human perceptual capacity of synesthesia that enables a person to hear colours as sounds and vice versa, for instance. He speaks rather of the very normal and fundamental quality of sensory percepts to penetrate each other and generate a fully existential experience that binds the world and the perceiver in an inseparable unity. They enable us to live in the 'flesh of the world', to use a powerful expression of Maurice Merleau-Ponty.[26]

Merleau-Ponty also argues strongly for the essential integration of the senses: 'My perception is [therefore] not a sum of visual, tactile and audible givens: I perceive in a total way with my whole being: I grasp a unique structure of the thing, a unique way of being, which speaks to all my senses at once.'[27] Bachelard calls this sensory interaction 'the polyphony of the senses'.[28]

Left

Van Eyck was one of the post-CIAM architects who aspired to reground contemporary architecture in its anthropological, existential embodied and mental soil: Aldo van Eyck, *Orphanage*, Amsterdam, 1956-60

Right

The body encounters the world as a multi-sensory experience: Pierre Bonnard, *Nude in the Bathtub*, 1936

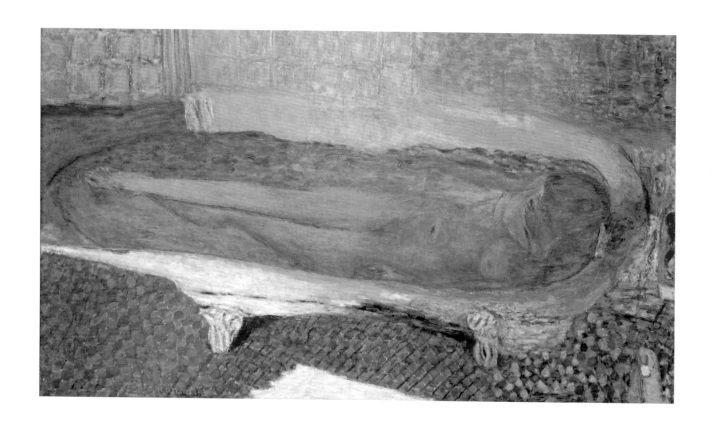

Confirming the philosophers' assumptions, modern research is exponentially expanding
our knowledge of the neurosciences, illuminating the extraordinary interconnectedness
and interactions of the various sensory areas of the brain.[29] The unexpected flexibility of
our sensory system has become especially evident in studies of the sensory capabilities
of the blind. 'The world of the blind, of the blinded, it seems, can be especially rich in
such in-between states – the intersensory, the metamodal – states for which we have
no common language', argues Oliver Sachs. 'And all of these… blend into a single
fundamental sense, a deep attentiveness, a slow, almost prehensible attention, a
sensuous, intimate being at one with the world which sight, with its quick, flickering,
facile quality, continually distracts us from.'[30]

The true miracle of our perception of the world is its very completeness, continuity and
constancy regardless of the fragmentary and discontinuous nature of our perceptions
through the different, seemingly incommensurable sensory channels. Normally we
manage to live in a unified and continuous world.

Experiencing Architecture

Although architecture has been and continues to be regarded primarily as a visual
discipline, spaces, places and buildings are apprehended as multi-sensory experiences.
Instead of seeing a building merely as a visual image, we confront it with all our senses at
once, and we live it as part of our existential world, not as an object outside ourselves. The
building occupies the same 'flesh of the world' as we do. Every building has its auditive,
haptic, olfactory and even gustatory qualities that give the visual perception its sense of
fullness and life.

Most importantly, an unconscious sense of touch is concealed in vision; through vision I
touch the materials, surfaces and edges of the building and judge their haptic qualities;
a building is experienced as inviting and pleasurable, or uninviting and aggressive
depending on these unconscious sensations. Significantly, the lack of architectural quality
is often more clearly experienced as a haptic rejection than a negative judgement of
the eye. Today's virtuoso structures may be exciting to the eye, but our comprehensive
existential sense often rejects them. We do not accept these buildings as the flesh of the
world in which we dwell.

When confronting a building I immediately occupy it through my unconscious bodily projections, and the building settles in me. Similarly, as I live in a city, the city dwells in me. There is an instant exchange; I become part of the architectural entity and it becomes part of me. A profound building offers me its aura and authority, whereas I project my emotions on to the building that projects them back to me.

In our role as architects we are confronted with a fundamental experiential duality: when encountering a live architectural entity, we immediately experience it in a multi-sensory manner as part of our life-world and it enters into a dialogue with our existential sense, historicity and memories, but in our design work we tend to be engaged with the visual, conceptual and abstracted qualities of the project. This divided architectural awareness seems to explain why our executed buildings often lack the humane qualities that we intended to put into the design. Historical and vernacular buildings have usually emerged directly in the lived world, or in a dense interaction with lived reality and the forces of tradition as opposed to the detached and distanced atmosphere of today's digitally operating architectural studio. In my view, even in the age of virtuality and virtual realities, the architect still needs to rely on the amazing human capacities of sensory experience and imagination. Only through our imaginative capacities are we able to conceive buildings in their multi-sensory and lived essence.

Instead of aestheticising buildings and manipulating sensory experiences, the task of architecture is to emancipate our senses and to strengthen our existential foothold and sense of reality. The sense of reality and self strengthened and poeticised by sensuous imagery is also capable of freeing our ability to dream, imagine and desire. Meaningful architecture always turns our attention away from itself back to the lived world, to ourselves, and to the realities of life.

Right

An artwork for all the senses:
Out early to work the cold
a wall of frozen snow
carved with a stick
almost through to the other side
collapsed in the sunlight
Izumi-Mura, Japan, 25 December 1987
Andy Goldsworthy

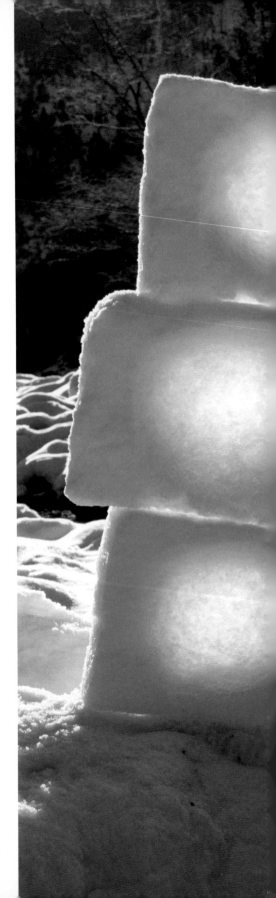

References

1   Italo Calvino, *Six Memos for the Next Millennium*, Vintage Books (New York), 1988, p 57.

2   Gaston Bachelard, *The Poetics of Space*, Beacon Press (Boston), 1969, p 46.

3   David Howes, 'Hyperesthesia, or the Sensual Logic of Late Capitalism', in *Empire of the Senses*, ed David Howes, Berg (Oxford and New York), 2005, pp 281-303.

4   Ibid. p 288.

5   Ibid.

6   The following books on the new sensory critique and awareness are recommended: Ashley Montague, *Touching: The Human Significance of the Skin*, Harpers & Row (New York), 1986; Diane Ackerman, *A Natural History of the Senses*, Vintage Books (New York), 1991; David Michael Levin, ed, *Modernity and the Hegemony of Vision*, University of California Press (Berkeley and Los Angeles), 1993; Martin Jay, *Downcast Eyes – The Denigration of Vision in Twentieth-Century French Thought*, University of California Press (Berkeley and Los Angeles), 1994; Georg Lakoff and Mark Johnson, *Philosophy in the Flesh, The Embodied Mind and Its Challenge to Western Thought,* Basic Books (New York), 1999; David Howes, ed, *Empire of the Senses,* Berg (Oxford and New York), 2005; Juhani Pallasmaa, *The Eyes of the Skin: Architecture and the Senses*, John Wiley & Sons (Chichester), 2005 (2nd edn).

7   Levin, ed, *Modernity and the Hegemony of Vision*, p 205.

8   'Architecture need do no more, nor should it ever do less, than assist man's homecoming.' *Aldo van Eyck*, in Herman Hertzberger, Annie van Roijen-Wortmann and Francis Strauven eds, *Stichten Wonen* (Amsterdam), 1982, p 65.

9   As quoted in *Not Architecture but Evidence that It Exists – Lauretta Vinciarelli: Watercolours*, Brooke Hodge ed, Harvard University Graduate School of Design (Cambridge, Mass) 1998, p 130.

10 Susan Stewart, 'Remembering the Senses' in Howes, *Empire of the Senses*, p 61.

11 The anthropology and spiritual psychology based on Rudolf Steiner's studies of the senses distinguish twelve senses: touch; life sense; self-movement sense; balance; smell; taste; vision; temperature sense; hearing; language sense; conceptual sense; and ego sense. Albert Soesman, *Our Twelve Senses. Wellsprings of the Soul*, Hawthorn Press (Stroud), 1998.

12 Heraclitus, Fragment 101a, as quoted in Levin, ed, *Modernity and the Hegemony of Vision*, p 1.

13 Plato, *Timaeus and Critias*, Penguin Books (London), 1977, p 47.

14 George Kubler, *The Shape of Time*, Yale University Press (New Haven, CT and London), 1962, p 14.

15   Stewart, 'Remembering the Senses', p 61.

16   Ibid, p 62.

17   Ibid, p 61.

18   Martin Jay, as quoted in Levin, ed, *Modernity and the Hegemony of Vision*, p 130.

19   Steven Connor, 'Michel Serres' Five Senses', in Howes, *Empire of the Senses*, p 322.

20   Michel Serres as quoted in ibid.

21   Wallace Stevens, 'Theory' in *The Collected Poems*, Vintage Books (New York), 1990, p 86.

22   As quoted in Bachelard, *The Poetics of Space*, p 137.

23   Connor, 'Michel Serres' *Five Senses*, p 323.

24   John Dewey, *Art As Experience*, Berkley Publishing (New York), 1980.

25   Ibid, pp 120 and 122-4.

26   Merleau-Ponty describes his notion of the flesh of the world in his essay 'The Intertwining – The Chiasm', in the *Visible and the Invisible*, ed Claude Lefort, Northwestern University Press (Evanston, IL), 1969. 'My body is made of the same flesh as the world…and moreover…this flesh of my body is shared by the world', p 248.

27   Maurice Merleau-Ponty, 'The Film and the New Psychology', in Maurice Merleau-Ponty, *Sense and Non-Sense*, Northwestern University Press (Evanston, IL), 1964, p 48.

28   Gaston Bachelard, *The Poetics of Reverie*, Beacon Press (Boston), 1971, p 6.

29   Oliver Sachs, 'The Mind's Eye: What the Blind See', in Howes, *Empire of the Senses*, p 33.

30   Jacques Lusseyran as referred to in ibid, p 36.

Druk White Lotus School, Ladakh, Northern Himalayas

Arup Associates: Holistic Design in a Climate of Extremes

Druk White Lotus School, Ladakh, Northern Himalayas
Holistic Design in a Climate of Extremes

The Druk White Lotus School is located in harsh and arid terrain. It draws its 350 pupils from the area surrounding the village of Shey, Ladakh, in a remote region of the Himalayas in Northern India. The school is a modest yet outstanding example of truly sustainable design conceived under the patronage of His Holiness the 14th Dalai Lama.

In contrast to conventional ways of working, the project was established to reflect traditional values and culture at a time when the community is under tremendous pressure to change. Working on site with the local committee for almost 15 years, Arup Associates and Arup have generated an architecture that retains the primacy of local formal and material traditions while integrating a setting for learning drawn from a modern transcultural experience.

This is an environment of extremes. At 3,500 metres above sea level, it is a high-altitude desert landscape. In this severe and fragile ecological context the development incorporates every available strategy to reduce resource consumption. Traditional materials are used: locally excavated stone, mud bricks, timber and grass. Walls contain outer leaves of hand-crafted granite blocks set in mud mortar. Traditional mud brick masonry is used internally, the whole providing increased thermal performance and durability in comparison to the local rendered mud brick equivalent.

The solidly earthquake resistant buildings rely on principles of natural ventilation, appropriate orientation and – for the residential buildings – trombe wall passive solar heating construction. The latest environmental engineering thermal and lighting analysis software is applied to design for minimised energy use. Water use is minimised too: for example, in modern versions of traditional dry latrines.

And yet the issues reach beyond the management of energy. Arup Associates' focus is an approach to design that maintains all components of humanity. Especially, the practice considers how human culture – tradition, religion, the intangible components of humanity – can be sustained in the face of modernity.

We believe that it is essential for architects and engineers to work in ways that prioritise individuals, promoting a sense of local identity: a response to the entire human experience, including the senses and memory. The aim is a process of whole life sustainability that puts people first; and that nurtures individual cultures – rather than creating universal models that expect people, cities and places around the world to behave identically.

Above
Wall painting, Shey, Ladakh

Previous page
The school draws 350 pupils from the villages of Shey, Leh and the surrounding region

Right
Granite walls define the boundary between desert and school

Our design tactics are entirely and radically collaborative, allowing free voice to local advocates of aspects of the projects – an integration of inputs, liberated of inappropriate influence from an externally imposed architectural vision. His Holiness the Dalai Lama was an enthusiastic partner: '…The idea of having a modern school which lays equal emphasis on the importance of preserving the valuable aspects of a traditional culture is very encouraging,' he commented. 'I have always believed in giving equal importance to both modern, scientific knowledge and traditional Buddhist culture.'[1]

Here in the Himalayan foothills, whole life sustainability has generated an architecture that is sensitive to unique cultural and spiritual values; nurturing them within a timeless design strategy that respects and maintains their worth indefinitely.

Reference

1   Brian Carter (ed), *Building Culture: The Druk White Lotus School: A Sustainable Model for Education and Design*, Buffalo Books (Buffalo, NY), 2006.

Above
Painted Mandala, Ladakh

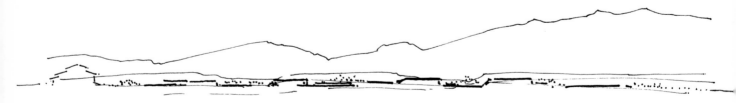

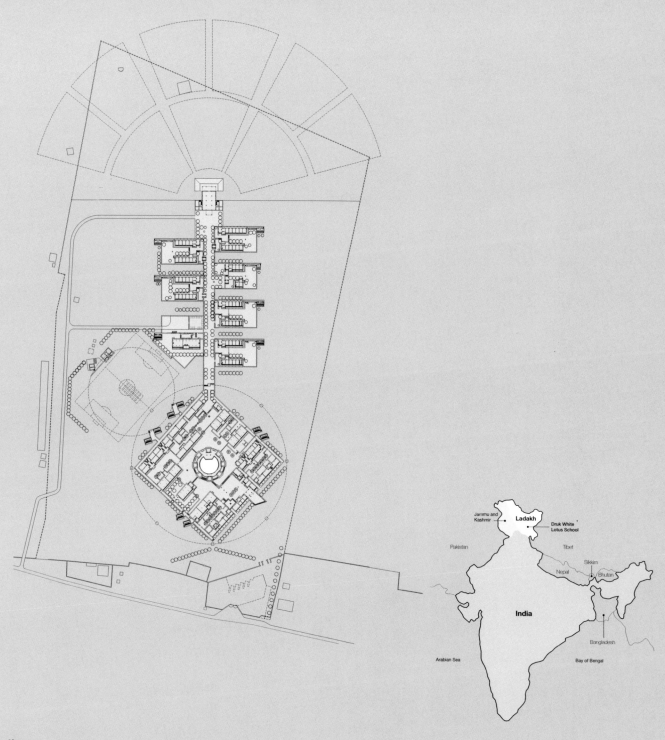

Above

Masterplan of school

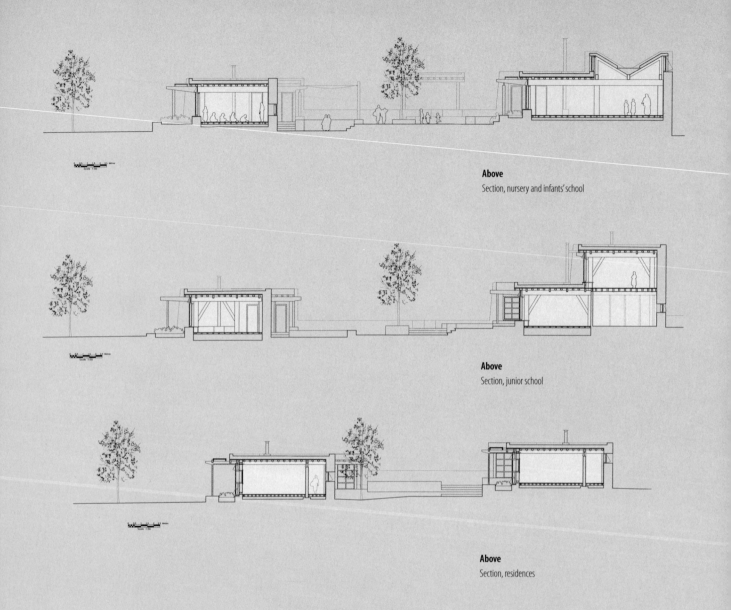

Above

Section, nursery and infants' school

Above

Section, junior school

Above

Section, residences

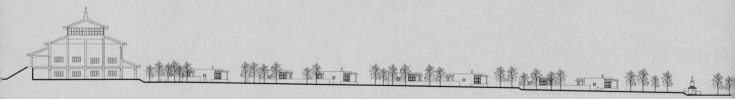

Above

Section through site along spine

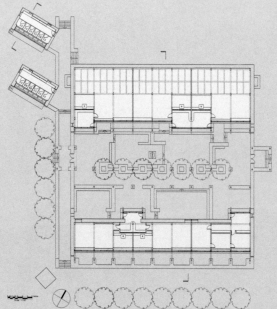

Above
Plan, nursery and infants' school

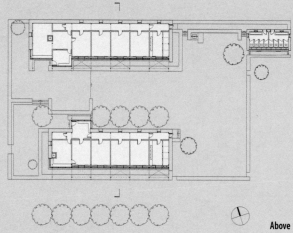

Above
Plan, residences

Left
The nursery and infants' school courtyard

Below
The junior school courtyard

Below
Children play under the school's entrance canopy

Left

School parent and child, Shey, Ladakh

Following pages

Daily transitions in a place of nurture

This page and opposite

The dining hall

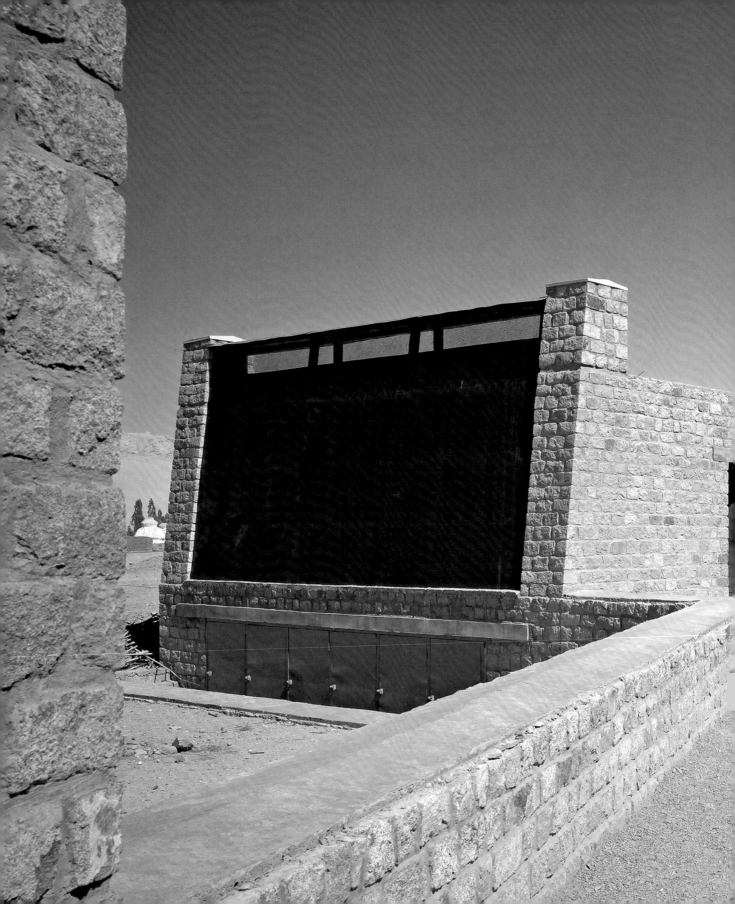

Previous page
The dry 'Ventilation Improved Pit' latrines use heat from the sun to drive a natural ventilation system. This both enhances sanitary conditions and assists the production of fertiliser from human waste.

Right
Carpenters' workshop

Below
The residential spine under construction

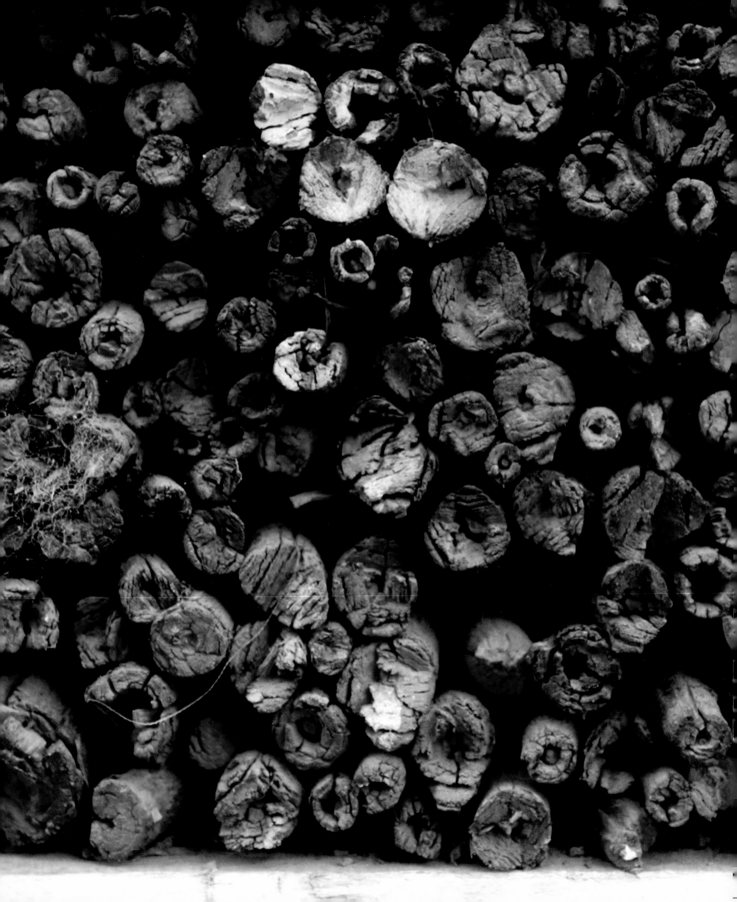

Leon van Schaik is Innovation Professor of Architecture at RMIT University, Melbourne. A great advocate of practice-based research, he has received awards for his services to architecture and education. His many published writings include *Design City Melbourne* (2005) and the forthcoming *Spatial Intelligence: New Futures for Architecture*, both published by John Wiley & Sons.

Spatial Intelligence and Place-Making

Leon van Schaik

All of us are born with capabilities that support several forms of Intelligence, conceived of as templates and refined over millennia of human evolution. Among these are our ability to perceive and navigate through space – 'Spatial Intelligence', and our awareness of space as we move through it – 'kinetic intelligence'. These two capacities are closely linked, highly developed, for example, in players of sports that combine movement with visualising of the spatial constraints of the game. And it is these same intelligences that we architects deploy intuitively when we design places – engage in what Arup Associates terms 'place-making'. We are not much aware of how spatial intelligence operates, it is consigned to the unconscious, and the 'mental space' that we individually and communally construct through using it is largely unexamined. This means that when we design, our place-making is informed by subconscious assumptions about what is good and what is not. Arup Associates' quest for better modes of place-making requires research into spatial intelligence and the way in which it is formed. This is difficult to do: the current mapping of the brain is locating those areas engaged by the exercise of our different intelligences, but the mental space that we construct can only be examined through introspection. Thus, the first step for the designer is to become attuned to his or her own 'mental space'. What follows is necessarily, therefore, a highly personal account of the construction of a layer of my 'mental space'.

Our spatial intelligence unfolds into the world, not in the abstract, but in places; and those places colour each individual's mental space.[1] Our language capability unfurls in an analogous way, common to us all but inflected by place into dialects. We become aware of our mental space only rarely, often shocked into recall by the surfacing of an 'eidetic' memory, a powerful moment of access to what are usually childhood experiences of wonder.[2] The most famous such recollection is of course Proust's madeleine, as he dipped it into tea, and himself into reverie. Sometimes in adult life a moment of wonder forges a new eidetic link in our mental space. Seeing the giant granite paving stones glowing in low sunlight in New York's SoHo was such a moment for me – a searing realisation that the streets of the capital of the New World being 'paved in gold' was not a metaphor, but an observation. Our mental space is in many ways a creature of our individual histories in space. We negotiate our way through the world using our mental space as our guide. Place makers – as this book recognises – have to grapple with designing receptors for multitudes of such spatial histories, some of which will be reassured by their designs, some shocked, some rendered indifferent. Here, illustrating the complex processes at work in the operating of our mental space, is an account of how some of my southern hemisphere mental space was re-forged by exposure to the northern hemisphere during my first years at university.

My first northern winter. Cold to the bone. A friend of a friend picks me up in a Morris Minor, the Grannie's car. He races us to Durham, sliding sideways in a four-wheel skid at every roundabout. Another spatial intelligence combined with another kinetic intelligence. We arrive at the Students' Union across a green from the cathedral. Snug inside the stone fastness we eat thick slabs of chocolate cake, drink steaming mugs of tea, and we warm up. Comfort restored we enter the cathedral and wander between its zigzag scoriated columns. In an instant I am transported back to my grandparents' house, 'Dunira', set in its wide gardens in the Natal Midlands. I am in the linen room, put to bed between cold, ironed sheets, a chill satin quilt promising warmth. Gingerly I uncurl, inching into the warmth my body has slowly generated. On the walls in a thick oak frame is a photograph of the columns of Durham Cathedral. An engraved metal plaque states simply: 'Midst massy pillars'.

Back on the Tyne, I am rowing on wide, choppy, steely and polluted water, through the most bridged stretch of river on earth. One of these bridges served as a quarter scale model for the Sydney Harbour Bridge – 'Have you seen our bridge?' they used to say, before the Opera House, in a time before 'modelling'. This stretch of river is a Piranesian collection of engineering beauty, silhouette framing silhouette in filters of grey light. Everyone in the team is from the Home Counties. They lose themselves in reverie. At school, two years before this, having lost our heat at Henley, we rowed back to Marlow through a long summer dusk, one luscious vista succeeding another in the verdant, thick river air. The Boathouse at Marlow stands alongside the Marlow Suspension Bridge, which served as a quarter scale model for the bridge between Buda and Pest. I find these miniature bridges as captivating as the Standard Vanguard Dinky Toy – a replica of his new car, which my father gave to me in the hospital when my tonsils were removed.

So, like a forgotten fire, a childhood can always flare up again within us.
Gaston Bachelard[3]

Left
Viewed from Macquarie Street, the Opera House reveals itself to be startlingly small, contrary to its iconic status: Jørn Utzon and Ove Arup & Partners, Sydney Opera House, 1957-73

We row through the gorge below the cathedral at Durham. The cox has the rudder hard to the right all the way around the hairpin bend. Before the bend, on a straight, a construction is going up on the banks, a double 'V' of concrete rises from a drum-like collar at water level on each side. On each 'V' is a 'U' tube of concrete. Later these are spun around to bridge between the cathedral promontory and Dunelm House, all cliff-hugging, concrete horizontals glazed randomly like La Tourette. Viewed from the side, they never seemed long enough, to reach across, the two arms of that bridge in the making. But they were. To walk across it was to re-dimension the space of the gorge in your mind, shrink it. The expansion joint is a 'U' and a 'T', the stem of the 'T' fitting precisely into the 'U' – town linked to university, said the designer. Facing the new bridge, we are in a 'spanking' new world; we are of the New World – studying under Richard Hamilton, we are 'Pop' babies. The designer of this bridge, Ove Arup, is now one of our heroes of the new, future world. My mental space is extended.

The city is restless, writes Declan O'Carroll, as he redefines the ethos of the practice. Multiple modernities form layers; generations of historical experience accrete. Take a look at the *Oxford Literary Guide to Great Britain and Ireland*[4] – at the maps that list every reference made to a place name. It tends to black. Take a look at the *Oxford Literary Guide to Australia*[5] – at the map that lists every reference made to a place name: a thin scattering of marks mostly around the edges. Then take a look at mappings – all tentative – of 'song-lines' across Australia,[6] and 40,000 years of experience track across the page. Stories repeated and repeated to forge 'abiding events'[7] that 200 years of conquest have not entirely dislodged.

And here we come, intent on 'place-making' rather than 'icon-chasing'. Feeling that, as Declan writes, due to the pervasive presence of the new media in our everyday lives: 'the traditional role of written text – of marking territory, of celebrating influential people and important events – has been lost.'[8] Hoping that we can now, through spatial information design, make up for the loss of that mode of communication, and testing this as in Arup Associates' design for a passageway – Plantation Lane – in the City of London[9] a throttling of the physical size and a virtual extension of the scale with an illuminated screen wall – we can begin again to mark and to inform territory.

Icons and landmarks are not architecture – they are objects, collectibles, subject to connoisseurship. Colin Rowe at Cornell spending an evening comparing the ogee curves of a dozen different Georgian chair legs. Like the Tempietto, they are scale-less and could be pepper pots or hotels in Bangkok. Objects that come in time to infect our memories, versions of the Eiffel Tower, the Golden Gate Bridge, Sydney Opera House. Unvisited they loom in the imagination, vast as pyramids. But my first glimpse of the Sydney Opera House around the

Above

Paddy Jupurrurla Nelson, Paddy Japaljarri Sims and Larry Jungarrayi
Spencer, *Yanjilypiri Jukurrpa (Star Dreaming)*, 1985

corner down Macquarie Street – quickened by my awareness that this structure too has on it
the hand of Ove Arup, the designer of my earliest structural love – revealed it to be startlingly
small. Almost something to hold in the palm of my hand. Like the car in the advertisement of
a 1956 issue of *National Geographic*, where in a snow storm an Oldsmobile is held cupped in
warm hands, promising to hold us in its turn, equally warm and safe. Impossible promise.

Yes, we experience space in a layered way, trailing our stories through it, marking it and
being marked by it. That corner of Melbourne where William Street crosses Collins Street,
where bunches of flowers in Cellophane have been taped to the pole that holds up the
overhead tram powerlines these past weeks; that mark where a brave man was shot,
intervening in a fight between a young woman and an armed man. It won't be the same
corner, ever again.

A brave venture, to enter into this layering, eschewing the easy target that is object
making. But an important venture, because without it we are neglecting the potentials
of our spatial intelligence and our closely related kinetic intelligence. We know more and
more about the neurology of these intelligences, less about their wholes. Especially we
now know that our memories function as 'projectories' – ceaselessly seeking to predict
future states that we are about to enter.[10] We probably cannot see anything anew. We are
always seeing that the new is like the old. Suffolk is rather like the Natal Midlands, don't
you think? My ancestors from Suffolk thought Natal was rather like Suffolk. Driving with
Gini Lee towards the Flinders Range in South Australia in mid summer, floating above the
dried out cellulose of the dead grassy plain, she asks: 'Isn't this like South Africa?' To which
I reply: 'Yes, except that if we were in the Highveld looking at such a scene through our
windscreen, we would know that it was mid winter out there, and bitterly cold. Whereas,
if we leave the car now, we will be in 40 degree heat. 'Like, but not like. Different. In new
situations we track through our mental space looking for matching patterns, and we can –
if we avoid the efforts of observing closely – make slipshod matches. This is trivial if we are
simply on a journey, but as place-makers this is unforgivably unprofessional. And yet we
architects do not expressly train ourselves in these capacities.

Tiger Woods tees up. He pulls his arms back, firmly clasped about his club. He takes a
swing. The camera pans down the vivid green slot of space between the oaks, a space
that seems to bend like a banana out of view around a corner over a tail of a lake. The ball
bounces onto the green. Rolls. A hole in one! What an astounding kinetic awareness of
space! What keen spatial intelligence! Flying north out of Tokyo, for half an hour all I can see
out of the airplane window are the worm carvings of fairways that have eaten up the forest

for 300 square kilometres. Thousands of people test their spatial intelligence against these banana slots everyday. They concentrate. They project. They float into their astral bodies to get a bird's eye view (they wish!).

We place-makers should do so too. If we did, would we have been party to the diminishing of the spatial environment of our fellows? At work most of them sit in sandwiches of space that are the same everywhere, 2.4 metres high, ceilings surfaced with fissured acoustic tiling punctuated by grids of rectangular light fittings, floors covered in carpet tiles. Windows far away, if any. If any, unopenable. They are scratchy, depressed. It's their work. It's their colleagues. Perhaps it's the unforgiving, minimally utilitarian, space?

Spatial and kinetic intelligence are the capabilities that architecture holds in trust for everyone. They are capabilities that are 'relegated to the humdrum' all too easily. So much so that most of us live most of our lives working in spaces that are bereft of any quality that could support ease of mind, comfort of body, well-being. And yet we do not protest. We accept symbol in place of substance, as an advertisement in *The Advertiser* in Adelaide declared: 'Where else except in Tuscany, could you find such a perfect Provencal villa?' So we collect images rather than seek out spaces. And city administrations vie with one another for the Guggenheim effect. These symbols lack content, leave us unsatisfied, and we fill them with technologies that make up for their inadequacies – air-conditioning and heating; home entertainment centres, sound systems, scented air. Our spatial intelligence is left unsatisfied, hunting for stimulus in all the wrong places.

How do we make spaces that satisfy spatial and kinetic intelligence? The first step is to acknowledge the existence of these capabilities. The second is to ensure that architects have a thorough understanding of the evolution of their own spatial histories – like really understanding a language, its literature, your dialect and its origins in Norse mythology or Greek legend. Rather as a psychoanalyst used to have to be psychoanalysed before being allowed to practice. So that you do not assume that what is 'comfort' or 'ease' to you, is 'comfort' or 'ease' to someone else who comes from a different community, has a different mental space derived from different spatial experience. Fully grounded, we can collaborate, consult. We can act as custodians of a knowledge that all of us have, but that most of us have internalised so deeply that we no longer pay it any conscious attention.

Those of us who have grown up in one country and have moved to another are forced into awareness of the workings of our spatial intelligence, because we cannot rely on the spatial assumptions that have been hard wired into us, synapse by synapse: our mental space.

Kinetically we are as at home – one golf course much like another. But sun on the ceiling in Newcastle on Tyne triggers a response set up in Waterkloof, Pretoria, and I leap out of bed set on diving into the pool for an early morning swim, only to be brought 'to my senses' as we say, brought back to my sensations of the actuality of a frosty day with sunlight bouncing into the room off frozen puddles. The surprise winds me. In adult life we seek out holidays in places that shock us into awareness of our spatial intelligence. New Yorkers whom I know fly to Bermuda and wade through silky air that strokes them back into a state of childhood wonder. Londoners drift on barges on canals through France, lulled into reveries that are as timeless as the long evenings of their soft childhoods. Isn't this the domain of place-making? Why does such 'centring' of the self only happen once or twice a year? Declan O'Carroll, in spaces like Plantation Lane, seeks to make places that put us in touch with ourselves every day of the week.

Sleep research is revealing how our off time is spent trawling through the happenings of the day, comparing them to the patterns we have forged in our intelligences, making adjustments where it seems useful, rejecting changes that seem aberrant, adjusting what we have been born with and has unfolded in one place with the experience of being in other places. Making 'weak' connections – as in the 'weak force' in physics – that the linear thinking of the wakened mind rules out. This, then, is why so many people find that 'sleeping on it' is an effective way to resolve complex problems. We have known this as 'common sense.' Now neurology maps how and where it happens in our minds. Recent research begins to break down the distinctions between spatial and kinetic intelligences, grappling with the evidence that 'mind' is a distributed system involving every cell in the body. It is not, after all, so fanciful to observe how physicists think better with chalk between thumb and forefinger, standing facing a blackboard, turning their backs on their audience, creating a spatial moment in the midst of a kinetic flow.[11]

Proust, as I noted earlier, was thrust into reverie by the taste of a madeleine. The smell of winter jasmine hurtles me into the laneways of Johannesburg. Taste, sight and smell. We are complex assemblages of such memories, and they persist – it now seems – because they are part of the way in which we negotiate the world we find ourselves in, a 'restless' world in which great cities contain large numbers of people who grew up in another country, wired up their spatial and language capabilities there, and now navigate a different world, building new neural connections as they go. Reading the city, all as surface[12] at first, then inflecting it with incident and depth.

Right
View inside the Costa surface 'dome': Minifie Nixon, Australian
Wildlife Health Centre, Healsville, Victoria, Australia, 2002-4

Below
3D modelling showing the form of the Costa surface: an importation
into architecture of a spatiality newly defined by mathematics.

Can space evolve? Are there new environments that are growing new recollections beyond the contingent rearrangements forced by topography and microclimate? You know – those inalienable qualities of space that lead my Swiss friends to complain that tomatoes bought in Como lose their taste as they are driven north across the border into the Ticino. That robbed the cheap red wine of its 'nose' as we took it home across the Channel to damper and cooler climes; that softened the baguette bought that morning, so that come evening all we had to offer our family and friends were travellers' tales. You should have tasted this in Paris! Architects Minifie Nixon have been importing into architecture spatialities newly defined by mathematics. At the Australian Wildlife Health Centre, they use a Costa surface as a new form of dome, one that initially perplexes with its inversions of what is inside, what outside. There are oculi open to the sky in three places as the Costa surface forms a circular ambulatory for viewing the operating theatres, and what seems a step into the outside at the centre – because the space rises up above the ambulatory – is in fact to step into a multimedia display. The Pantheon in Rome has an oculus that is remorseless in its structural and poetic logic, an invention 2,000 years old, and still fresh to experience. Something of that quality inheres in the Costa surface, applied so aptly to the public programme in the Healsville animal medical centre. It eludes photography. You have to be there to experience its challenge to our sense of the norm, its re-awakening of our awareness of our spatial intelligence.

Designing with this knowledge of how we inhabit the world diminishes the importance of the canon in architecture, makes a trivial pursuit of the ambition to create a new icon that extends or shatters that canon – an arcane collection of objects nursed by those 'in the know', professionals who have become a priesthood protecting mysteries. There is another way. The place-making way. It begins with us acknowledging Bachelard's central intuition: 'Thus we fill the universe with drawings we have lived.'[13] And obeying his central injunction: 'Each one of us then should speak of our roads and our roadside benches.' Thus we equip ourselves to design as Arup Associates has at Plantation Lane, a space in the city that sets out to play with our spatial intelligence rather than to place an obstacle in its path.

Today we spend much time navigating virtual space in information environments. We are only beginning to apply our spatial intelligence to this, confronting in the main terrains that have been conceived of as a desktop and a filing cabinet. When we engage spatially, all too often we are confined to the insides of a torus, drifting through sensations in an endless loop. Space travel, we incongruously call this. Games thrust us kinetically against spaces that are sketchy simulacra of actual worlds. But in these repeated thrustings we can observe spatial

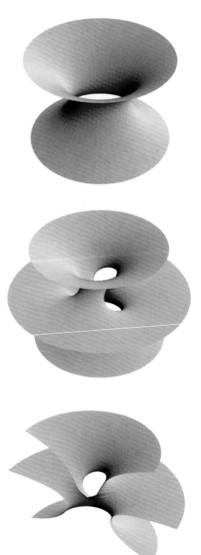

Left
Sir Ove Arup visits the Kingsgate Footbridge in Durham
during construction in 1963

Left
Interlocking device on the swing bridge: the expansion joint is
a 'T' and a 'U' – town linked to university

and kinetic intelligence at work together building the thin synapses of games. In the virtual environment of 'Second Life', an on-line meeting place, we can design places and ourselves. We encounter little resistance, and the actuality we engender is thin and over-stated. We create fantasy islands and populate them with avatars of ourselves: caricature lands.

Can the information surface with which hyperspace promises to surround us deliver more than this? Or is our spatial intelligence hungry for more substantial information? Taste, touch, texture, rhythm, sound, light shifting through the day, colour – that panoply identified by Rasmussen.[14] Rasmussen who understood so well how we can see softness in what is actually hard, can feel hardness in what is seemingly soft. Should we complement the actualities of making with images of what we can see in space, rather than make spaces that are so lit that the universe is always visible in our cities on clear nights, as close as it palpably is in the few dark places left in the world? In remote locations it comes naturally to make places that are expressive of the actions that made them. Adzed wooden surfaces reveal the hands that have worked, and we read that. Stone walls embed the act of their making, and we read it in the lodgings of each stone relative to its neighbours, aware of the thinking that has brought it into being in just this spot, and no other. Architects concerned with place do well to understand the power of the act of placement.[15] Arup Associates' Druk White Lotus School is suffused with this knowledge. At Plantation Lane it is most evident in the plan. Architect Robert Simeoni, currently researching the nature of his architectural mastery with me, works with fashion designers as he seeks out ways to keep the traces of making in his finished work, so that we are always aware of the effort and the ingenuity that has gone into the making. If we want to work with spatial intelligence – if we want to alert people to their spatial intelligence – then we need place-making, place revealing architecture, far more than we need collections of icons.

Back in the gorge at Durham, following Arup's design, an object is constructed on each side of the river, aligned with the river so as not to obstruct its flow, or the flows of activity up and down its course and along its banks. The object has an iconic form – in elevation like a hand with fingers coned up, supporting a tray. Then, completed, the object is turned to sit at right angles to the river, and it becomes a space, its iconic form now only visible to those passing below. And so apt is this vector of space in this place that it is as if, like the cathedral, it has always been there.

Left
Durham Cathedral viewed across the gorge, showing the swing bridge making landfall in the shadow of the cathedral

References

1   Howard Gardner, *Intelligence Reframed. Multiple Intelligences for the 21st Century*, Basic Books (New York), 1999.

2   Philip Fisher, *Wonder: The Rainbow and the Aesthetics of Rare Experiences*, Harvard University Press (Cambridge, MA), 1998.

3   Gaston Bachelard, *The Poetics of Reverie: Childhood, Language, and the Cosmos*, trans. Daniel Russell, Beacon Press (Boston), 1971 p 104.

4   Dorothy Eagle and Meic Stephens, eds, *The Oxford Literary Guide to Great Britain and Ireland*, Oxford University Press (Oxford), 1993 (2nd edn).

5   Association for the study of Australian Literature, map compiled from the *Oxford Literary Guide to Australia*, Oxford University Press (Oxford), 1987.

6   Bruce Chatwin, *Songlines*, Penguin (London), 1988.

7   Tony Swain, *A Place for Strangers, Towards a History of Australian. Aboriginal Being*, Cambridge University Press (Melbourne), 1993.

8   Paul Brislin, ed, *Plantation Lane: Time and Tide*, Wordsearch (London), 2005, p 24.

9   Ibid.

10   Jessica Marshall, 'Future Recall', *New Scientist* (24 March 2007), pp 436-40.

11   Leon van Schaik, *Mastering Architecture: Becoming a Creative Innovator in Practice*, John Wiley & Sons (Chichester), 2005.

12   Paul Carter, *Living in a New Country : History, Travelling and Language*, Faber and Faber (London), 1992; and Paul Carter, 'Migrant Musings: Christmas in Brunswick', *Agenda* (Melbourne), 1992.

13   Gaston Bachelard, *The Poetics of Space*, Beacon Press (Boston), 1969, republished 1994 with the subtitle 'The Classic Look at How We Experience Intimate Places'.

14   Steen Eiler Rasmussen, *Experiencing Architecture*, Chapman & Hall (London), 1959.

15   Victoria Newhouse, *Art and the Power of Placement*, Monacelli Press (New York), 2005. Remarkable account of the kind of space curation that Declan O'Carroll argues for, but in the context of art and museums.

Part Three considers the implementation of unified design in practice. A visual essay shows how the **collaborative engineering** of an architecture forms the essence of people-centred design. Finally, selected Arup Associates projects articulate the themes explored in this text.

THREE

DESIGNING THE WHOLE

Unified design is a dynamic collaborative invention. Our starting point is free of any preconceived signature language.

Our creative process is agile and provocative, an improvisational approach that celebrates the potential of each opportunity.

Pan-disciplinary speculations capture the influences that emerge from a multiplicity of origins, ultimately converging into a multilayered whole.

Our studio is a learning society underpinned with an intellectual and creative desire to explore new techniques, exploit new technologies, discover new solutions. Always with a humble sense of purpose: to positively transform people's life experience – and to inspire and delight.

Collaborative Engineering

Arup Associates

Collaborative Engineering
Arup Associates

Ove Arup believed that only the closest integration of disciplines could produce beautiful, harmonic forms; economical and fit for purpose. Traditional engineering and architectural relationships are often an oscillation: drawings pass back and forth, gradually reaching refinement. In contrast, at Arup Associates, teams of architects and engineers deliver buildings from a single studio. The creative process is faster, more akin to fusion. Quick feedback times generate opportunity for multiple paths of investigation. But it's the creative fusion, especially under pressure, that adds a magical extra ingredient.

Unified design extends the collaborative approach radically and laterally: it maximises the potential of collective creativity. Engineers are liberated to lead the discovery of new languages; to explore the unexpected.

Collective Creativity

Intense integration allows each discipline to reach beyond the boundary of its typical role, to develop holistic design solutions. Partners range from sustainability engineers to psychologists and artists, in the belief that confident, diverse viewpoints generate surprising results. The success of this approach is especially visible in highly complex building types such as the Citi data centre in Frankfurt, or the Sky television recording and transmission facility, both under construction. Typically, each building type is a huge energy consumer, yet both are examples of the most sustainable buildings of their genre in the world; a result generated by the added value of disciplines that work beyond their calling. Boundaries are blurred, creating opportunity to develop design solutions – such as the naturally ventilated studios – that neither client nor architect could have anticipated at the outset.

The Human Interface

Scale, texture, touch: detail brings humanity to architecture. It is difficult for people to relate to whole buildings, but not to their more immediate context and experiences. Richness and accessibility lie in the connections and junctions and interfaces. Yet detail is only one part of the fugue: as important is the relationship of the detail to the whole. Structural engineering brings form and scale and an underlying rhythm to spaces, an antidote to alienation and displacement. Architects and engineers need to care passionately about the expression of structure and its details.

Total architecture implies that all design decisions have been considered together. . . artistic wholeness or excellence depends on it.

Ove Arup, Key Speech, 1970[1]

How people interact with their environment – how safe we feel, our control over comfort, the length of time before we can effect change in our environment – are also fundamental. We act individually and in smaller groups. Research shows that up to six or seven people will work together to reach a compromise regarding comfort conditions in open plan offices. By understanding these issues, we can engineer better places, with more satisfied and productive people working and living in them.

The environmental analogy of the termite hill as a metaphor for the high thermal-mass cooling of a building only tells half the story. It is the termites that block and unblock the air paths, track the sun and then open and close the vents. Without the termites, the hill is a stale and stagnant place. This analogy extends to buildings where the relationship between people, building physics and control systems has broken down. And it is here that environmental engineers are the dynamic interface between people and their environment.

Building environments are perceived as systems in constant flux, always linked to the human sensory experience; and to people's mood and wellbeing. This interface is fundamental to the creation of satisfying, low-impact places in which people can live, work and play. To weave human experience into a design; to maximise the opportunity for people to fulfil their potential: these are the environmental engineer's responsibility and vocation.

Integral Sustainability

Advances in design and construction technology make it possible to construct almost any iconic form the architectural imagination can conceive. But a gratuitous approach to architecture is unacceptable: designers have to respond to site constraints and natural drivers – such as the embodied and actual energy consumed by projects.

This doesn't mean that sustainability is an end in itself. Nor is it an optional bolt-on. It is a natural by-product of integrated, functional design. Unified design considers the impact of any architectural solution on the operational life of the project, to provide the best environment with the least impact on the planet's resources. Even more, designs must deliver whole life sustainability. They must reinforce individual cultures and traditions, and stand firm against a homogenising modernity.

Ultimately, unified engineering has one specific purpose: better design for people. Design that has meaning in its part and whole is responsive to human and planetary needs;

and where technology is not an end in itself, but is trained in the service of ecologically sensitive, efficient spaces. Engineering is no support role. Unified design frees engineers to lead this process of creative discovery.

Collaborative Engineering in Practice

Clearly, the experience of the built environment has a profound effect on individuals and society. Recently the engineer's role in the setting of successful parameters has been well established at master plan scale; for example, in projects such as Stratford City and Dongtan. Here, sustainability frameworks devise the spaces and the rules within which zones, plots and buildings are later created by teams of designers, constructors and occupiers. When we create new cities, or regenerate parts of others, it is so important that the underlay is set by intertwined systems: ecological paths, energy, water, transport and waste. Of course, the buildings themselves must play their part in the whole. This integration is no longer optional for mankind – the ecological consequences that face us can only be addressed by holistic, future-proofed infrastructures.

As an essential component of unified thinking, the engineering mind must necessarily become expansive and inclusive; and must be able to interrogate complex ideologies for a comprehensive solution to a particular context and situation. How can we use the master plan to buffer public space from rail noise? What emerging technologies do we need to plan for? Can we reuse all the demolition waste? How low-carbon can we go? What is the least amount of structure we can use? How can we create sunlit, vibrant and exciting places to be? What about the production and transport of food?

It is the ability to envision and then design the answers to these large-scale questions that drives environmental impact towards 'better', rather than 'less bad', and that engages people's energies to achieve a more rewarding, lower impact lifestyle.

The Art of the Impossible?

The strength of the individual disciplines is an essential precursor to a successful collaboration – enquiry, research, innovation, learning and leadership. Partners in the collaboration have to demand the best of each other, to push beyond normal comfort levels. We must ask, for the project, the discipline and the individual – is it good enough? Is it bold enough?

This remains an ongoing challenge for unified design. To maximise the potential for the design outcome, the team must embrace the very best of each diverse contribution, no matter how complex or potentially controversial. This necessarily involves evolution of ideas over time, but also the injection of new people, new ideas and points of view. To challenge each individual within a collaborative framework requires creative tension – only the best thrive with this level of design commitment. In this context, engineers are no longer serving a singular idea set by others. Instead, they are fundamental creators of the vision from the outset.

Reference

1   Ove Arup's key speech originally published in *Arup Journal*, London, December 1970.

Axial forces in primary arches

Self weight deflection

Imposed load deflection

Above and below

The three primary arches traverse different, mutually
supporting planes, providing significant strength
and stiffness with light steel members

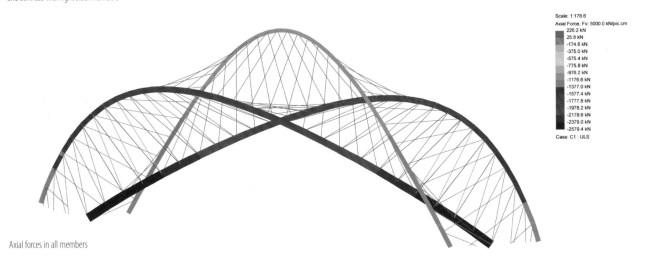

Scale: 1:178.6
Axial Force, Fx: 5000.0 kN/pic.cm

226.2 kN
25.8 kN
-174.6 kN
-375.0 kN
-575.4 kN
-775.8 kN
-976.2 kN
-1176.6 kN
-1377.0 kN
-1577.4 kN
-1777.8 kN
-1978.2 kN
-2178.6 kN
-2379.0 kN
-2579.4 kN

Case: C1 : ULS

Axial forces in all members

Sheffield Footbridge

Shortlisted; Competition, 2008

An efficient parabolic arch form is created from a simple triangular prism section, which rotates as it spans a road. This generates 'spiralling' chords and a warped soffit surface. Together, these appear as a pair of intersecting stainless-steel blades, especially when illuminated from beneath at night. The form was devised as a structurally economic, distinctive gateway to represent the harmony of the joined communities of Sheffield and Rotherham.

Below

The muted lighting scheme is designed to limit energy demand to levels that can be provided by renewable energy sources, such as PV or wind

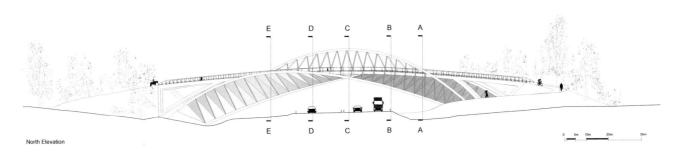

North Elevation

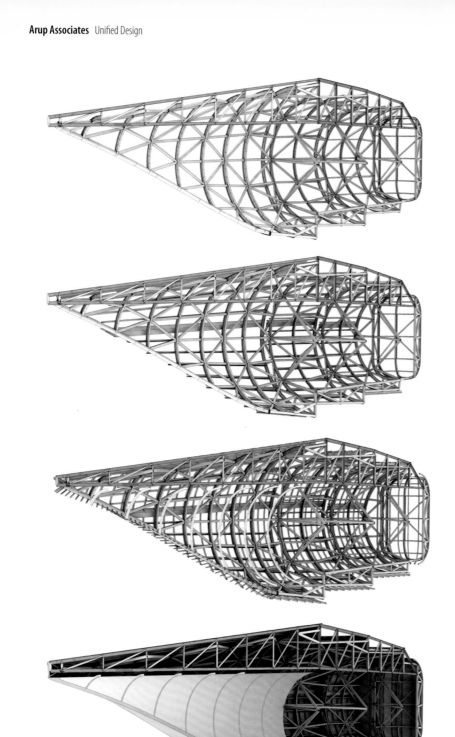

Primary, secondary and tertiary steel members

Kensington Oval Cricket Pavilion, 2007

In the tropical environment of Barbados, a steel cowling acts as a wind scoop to catch even the most gentle breezes. It provides comforting cross-ventilation to spectators, and protects upper seating tiers from sun and rain. Aerospace-style frame and skin construction resolves the double-curved form. The large-scale dynamic shape provides a sense of importance for the main pavilion, and announces the presence of this cricketing 'institution' within the urban setting of Bridgetown.

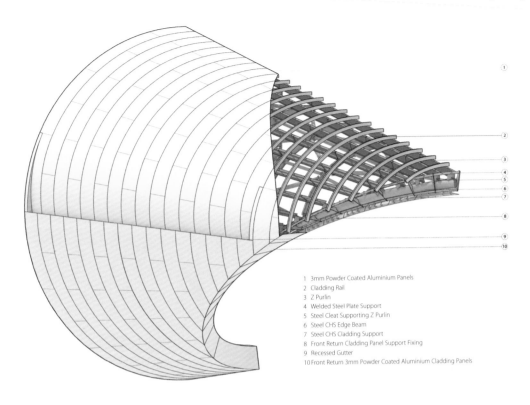

1 3mm Powder Coated Aluminium Panels
2 Cladding Rail
3 Z Purlin
4 Welded Steel Plate Support
5 Steel Cleat Supporting Z Purlin
6 Steel CHS Edge Beam
7 Steel CHS Cladding Support
8 Front Return Cladding Panel Support Fixing
9 Recessed Gutter
10 Front Return 3mm Powder Coated Aluminium Cladding Panels

1 3mm Powder Coated Aluminium Precut and Rolled Panel
2 Recessed Self-tapping Surface Cladding Fixing
3 Rubber Gasket
4 Extruded and Rolled Aluminium Cladding Rail
5 Aluminium Cladding Rail Support ±20mm Tolerance
6 Moisture Barrier
7 Cladding Panel Fixing Plate
8 Z Purlin
9 Steel Supporting Structure

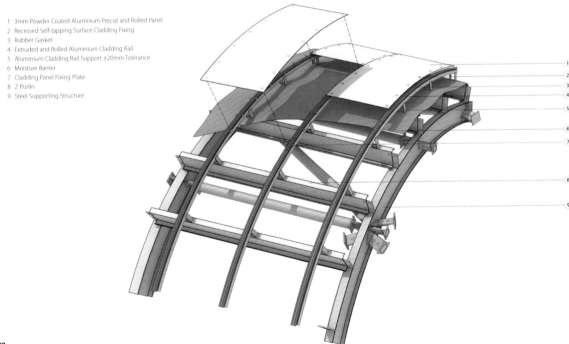

Above

Cladding components

Above and left
Advanced high-efficiency hybrid photovoltaic cladding combines
ultra-thin amorphous silicon with monocrystalline technology in one
cell – an optimum solution for London's cloudy skies. Covering over
200 square metres of the upper surface of the long cantilevers, the
cladding delivers a substantial proportion of the bus station's energy
demand: a measured annual output of almost 27 megawatt hours

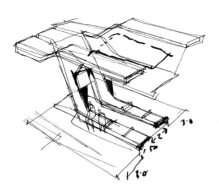

Vauxhall Transport Interchange, 2005

The dramatic 'super-long' cantilever of this
stainless-steel ribbon is an urban landmark and
a symbol of integrated sustainability. The upper
surface of the cantilever is clad with a photovoltaic
array to generate supplementary power for
the building, and is oriented at precisely the
appropriate angle to maximise power generation
from the London sky. Undulations along the length
of the canopy reflect the frequency of bus stands.
Each dip provides a seating refuge that enhances
and provides amenity for the local environment.

This page
Development of the stainless-steel clad 'ribbon',
from earliest sketch to construction

British Waterways Headquarters
Project, 2006

The entire building 'floats' above the ground to overcome numerous constraints at surface level. This introduces a new pedestrian route to the adjacent canal, and provides a public interface for the company. It also allows the structure to reach out above the water, to greet visitors arriving by boat. The floating headquarters uses the façade as a giant truss, which enables the building to span between cores without any other support. The depth of the truss façade is articulated by integrated natural ventilation openings.

Below and right

The proximity of structural members expresses the variation in forces along the truss, and provides a dynamic and honest articulation of the façades

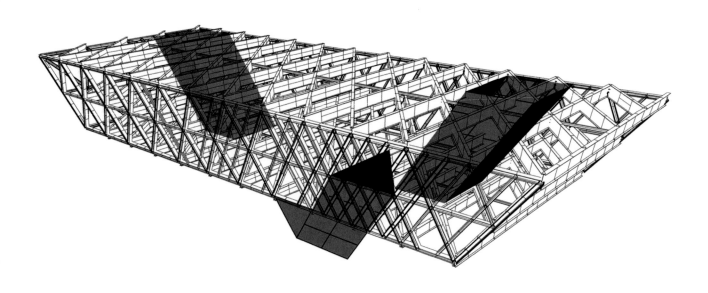

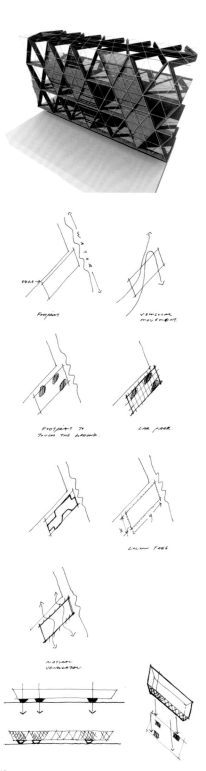

Above
Concept principles

Plantation Place Glass Bridge, 2004

The design requirement to provide an almost
invisible suspension bridge was resolved by the
unusual use of glass in compression. Rectangles
of structural glass fit closely between the steel
tensile elements to provide a translucent floor.
The blocks of glass take up the diagonal forces
in the structure, and remove any tendency
of the bridge to 'rack', or distort. The resulting
structure is almost entirely transparent, and yet
has no discernible sway or vibration.

Biomimetics, 2006

Produced by Arup Associates for the BBC documentary *Biomimetics*, the animation stills, **above**, illustrate the potential for biomimetic design processes to result in new design languages that learn from the solutions provided by nature.

The Plantation Place, **left**, is challenged to shade itself only when it needs to. Here, the human skin's local release of tanning agents is the biomimetic technique used to inform a technological response – in this case, hundreds of sensors operate shades only when locally stimulated by sunlight.

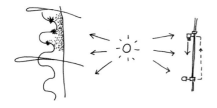

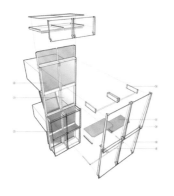

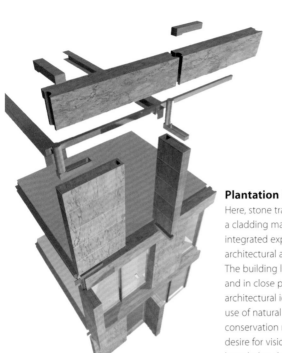

Plantation Place South, 2004

Here, stone transcends its common use as a cladding material. Instead, it provides an integrated expression of the building's structural, architectural and environmental concerns. The building lies within a conservation area and in close proximity to a Wren church. The architectural identity relies significantly on the use of natural stone. At the same time, energy conservation needs to be balanced with the desire for vision glazing. These considerations have led to the evolution of a load-bearing, self-shading façade, wrought from natural stone.

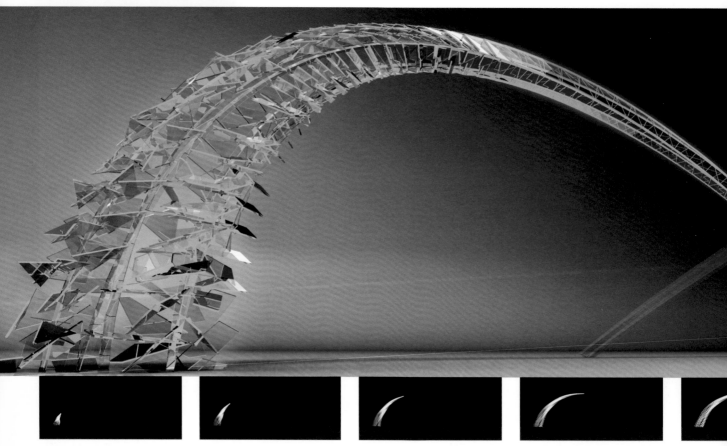

Above

Trajectory of construction sequence

Right

1 Rocket trajectory equates to 2 parabolic arch

3 Tsiolovsky's rocket equation compares to 4 compression
and asymmetric bending in an arch

5 Rocket flight profile compares to 6 structural widths of a tapered arch, fixed at one end

7 Stages of a rocket flight path compare to 8 stages of arch construction

Rocket Junction

First Place; Competition, 2006

The design concept for this gateway structure derives from the flight path of a rocket, symbolic of the local area's regenerative transition from the industrial age to the space age. The parabolic trajectory provides an efficient spanning structural form. The metaphorical thrust plume of the accelerating rocket tapers from the launch site to its destination: correlating perfectly with the bending moment of a tapered arch, fixed at one end.

The competition-winning scheme was developed in collaboration with artist Simon Patterson. It is sited close to the track where the first modern locomotive – George Stephenson's *Rocket* – was trialled.

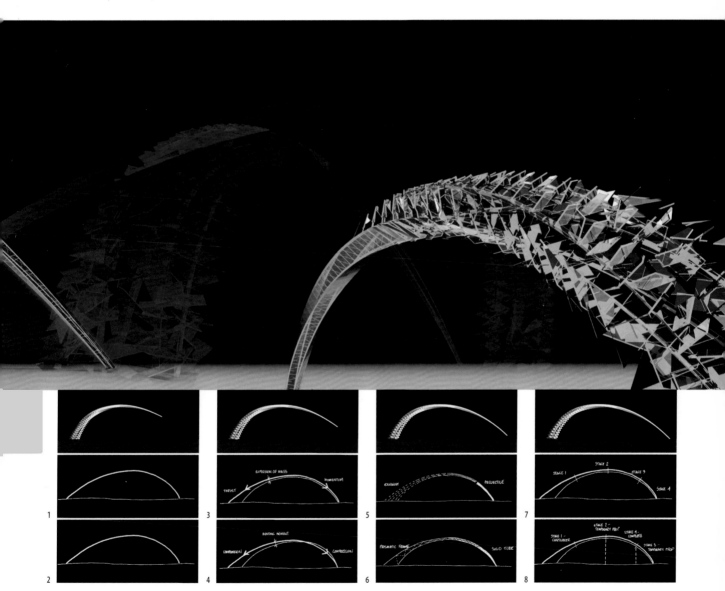

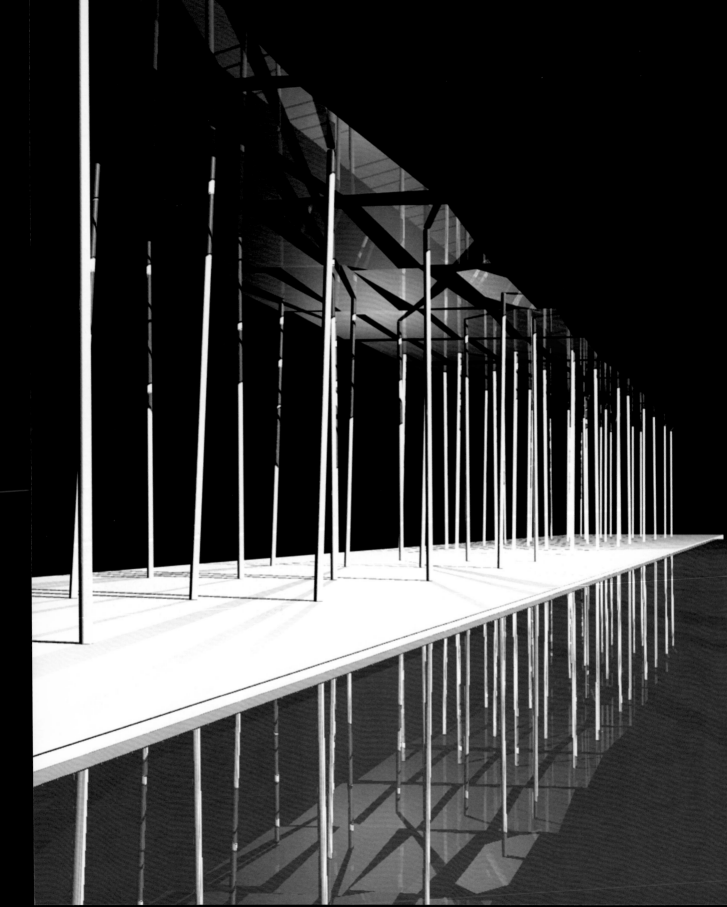

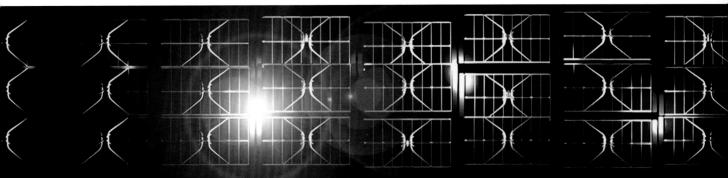

Cambridge Colonnade
Project, 2004

Through the process of biomimesis, the technological design solution for this canal-side walkway shelter echoes the characteristics of a natural waterside microclimate. Slender steel 'tree trunks' support photovoltaic panels. These slender structures provide a canopy that sways gently in the wind, its reflection rippling in the water. The swaying motion is damped by interconnecting springs that absorb kinetic energy. At night, this wind energy adds a firefly effect to the general illumination provided by the solar powered photovoltaic array.

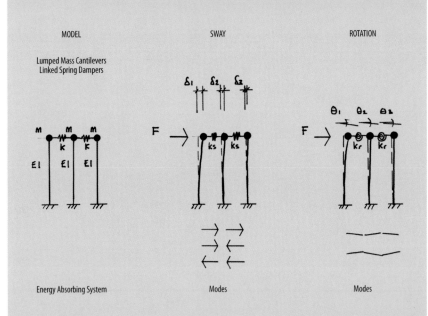

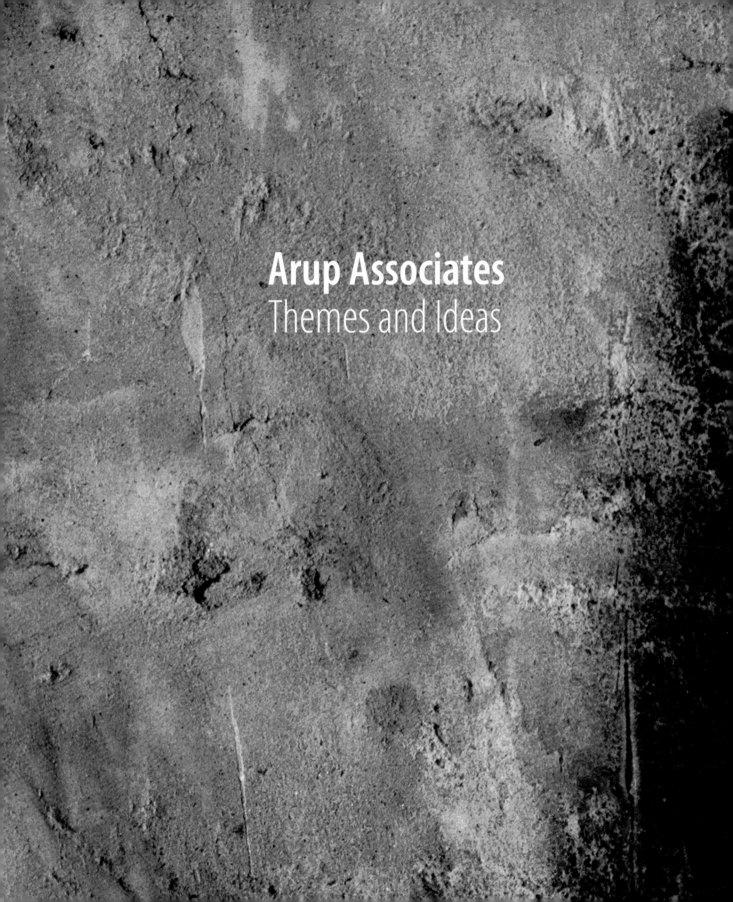

Arup Associates
Themes and Ideas

Arup Campus

Solihull, UK

2007

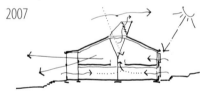

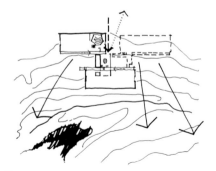

Top
Weathered timber cladding integrates building and landscape

Above and right
The natural ventilation strategy defines the form of the building

The appearance of the Arup Campus building reflects a radical traditionalism – a rational approach to the rural vernacular that surrounds this project. The weathering of the timber cladding melds the building into its landscape. Towering above the eaves, giant roof pods are prominently expressed. These distinctive elements define the ethos of an environmentally responsible and responsive space – a gentle, sustainable office building, designed for people.

The structure has an unusually wide plan. Despite this, the building is designed to be naturally ventilated and to maximise daylight penetration. The roof pods provide the solution. Through a chimney-like stack effect they drive the ventilation naturally and bring controlled daylight deep into the heart of the building. This low-energy strategy is supported by the thermal mass of the exposed concrete floor and roof soffits. Exposed hard surfaces might cause unpleasant reverberation, but sound absorption within the volume is provided by specially designed dampers integrated into the light fittings. Externally, the contextual timber louvres control solar gain and glare, and provide human-scale detail to the façade. Moreover, the louvres and opening windows can be manually operated, giving back environmental control to the individuals who live in the building.

The two-storey building is laid out as two long pavilions, sited to relate to the contours of the land. The slope, used to reduce on-site cut and fill and to enhance the relationship between the workplace and the external landscape beyond, also allows the creation of internal half levels and atria that ensure a fluid connectivity between the work spaces.

This deceptively simple building is driven by a better, more humane response to the workplace. At Arup Campus, energy efficiency, good internal communication and a sense of user control are all the end results of an expressive unified design.

Pema Karpo Library, Druk White Lotus School

Ladakh, Northern India

Completion 2010

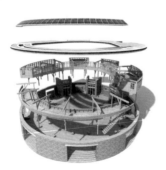

Top
Interior view of the central courtyard

Above
Exploded axonometric

The masterplan of the Druk White Lotus School is inspired by the Mandala: a series of buildings is organised around courtyards that fuse the practical functions of the school with this symbol of the cosmos (see diagram, p 58). A new library building will eventually enclose the centremost courtyard. It is named after Mipham Pema Karpo, a great Tibetan scholar born in 1527 and the direct spiritual ancestor of the school founder, the 12th Gyalwang Drukpa.

The library and central courtyard are modelled on elements of the Buddhist symbol of the Dharma Wheel, which represents the unity of all things. The mass of the library creates arcaded and sheltered areas. Its courtyard is entered via one of eight gateways, the spokes of the Dharma Wheel, which allow informal movement of children and teachers into the flexible space beyond. This circular courtyard is a Cora route, for ritual recitation and prayer; a space for teaching and performance, and a place for the market stalls to set up on school open days. Exhibition and archive rooms face the courtyard. Above, an overlooking balcony provides access to the library: the wisdom of Dharma.

In keeping with the strategies developed for the school as a whole, the library design embodies sustainable thinking. It is oriented to maximise daylight into the courtyard and building. Heating is provided entirely by solar gain, and curtains are drawn to prevent glare. The library space is entered from lobbies designed to conserve heat, while the traditional mud roof provides good thermal and acoustic properties. Solar panels will provide power for computers and lighting.

The timber panelling and glazing to the library have been chosen to contrast with the granite walls that enclose the courtyard. Building materials are mostly indigenous, and supplies of sustainable resources are closely audited. Local expertise is fundamental to the design of the detailing and the symbolic aspects of the architecture.

The Pema Karpo Library will promote both international and local art, science, language and religion. It represents the centrepiece of a design philosophy of whole life sustainability: an approach to people focused design that measures the conservation of energy as equal to the conservation of human culture.

Above
The library balcony

Right
Internal view of the library

City of Manchester Stadium

Manchester, UK

2002 Commonwealth Games

2003 Manchester City Football Club

The stadium is the focus of a far wider regeneration programme that has provided sport and leisure facilities in a previously challenged environment. It is built on a contaminated brownfield site for a remarkably low budget, and the distinctive architecture has been created from those parts essential to the function of the facility. Access ramps spiral around concrete towers. These house plant, but also carry the roof masts and stabilise the building. The undulating 'saddle shape' roof, which covers every seat, is supported by an innovative pre-stressed cable net that made provision for a special feature of the building: phased construction of the roof, at first for athletics and then later for football. The City of Manchester Stadium was centrepiece and host to the 2002 Commonwealth Games. Now in its legacy role, it has been the home of Manchester City Football Club since 2003.

This is a place for people. Special consideration has been given to efficient operation, spectator comfort and security. In particular, disabled access and viewing facilities are exceptional. The circular building perimeter combines with an optimal 'TV shaped' seating plan to create elevations that sweep up from the north and south to contain the upper stands on the east and west sides. These high sides not only provide protection from the prevailing winds and low sun angles, but also serve to concentrate the seats in the areas most favoured by spectators. In turn, the low south stand allows sunlight onto the pitch, creating optimum viewing and playing conditions.

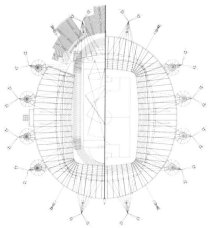

Plan
Commonwealth Games mode (LHS); Manchester City mode (RHS)

Top
Manchester Stadium in its Commonwealth Games format. The flexible design allowed the addition of extra tiers for legacy use by Manchester City Football Club

Right
Built on a contaminated brownfield site, the stadium is integral to the local regeneration programme

Above and right
City of Manchester Stadium is a theatre of sport, and a
design for people, both in its guise as a cultural arena
for the Commonwealth Games; and in its legacy role
as a stadium for Manchester City Football Club

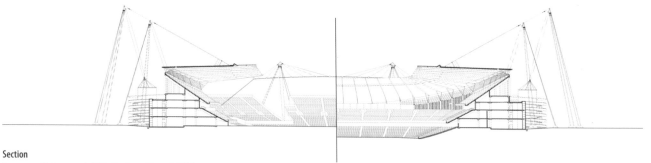

Section
Commonwealth Games mode (LHS); Manchester City mode (RHS)

Kensington Oval

Bridgetown, Barbados
2007

At Kensington Oval, the West Indies resisted test match defeat for 49 years. Considered one of the greatest grounds in the world, this is the historic home of West Indies cricket. Its importance stems from uniquely enthusiastic spectators, the responsive wicket, and the memorable performances of teams and individuals.

In 2007 the West Indies hosted the ICC Cricket World Cup and Arup Associates was appointed to redevelop Kensington Oval in preparation for the finals. Unusually, the ground is made up of individual stands, not a stadium. Although over 80 per cent of the existing stands were replaced, the new development maintains this important distinction.

Each stand has a specific character, and new stands retain the positive attributes of those they replace. The final scheme maintains the intimate character of the ground, creating a vibrant new facility. The inclusion of a mound stand and a pool adds atmosphere to the already rich West Indian cricket culture.

The redesigned facility is not only sensitive to the particular sporting cultures of the region – it acts as a significant urban catalyst for the surrounding areas of Bridgetown too. Previously, the ground had a limited urban presence. This was rectified by the creation of new civic spaces, along with a mixed-use development that provides year round, non-match day activities.

Above and below
The distinctive form of the 3W's Stand is driven by
practical function: it acts as a wind scoop, to provide
both cross-ventilation and sun protection

Imperial College

London, UK
2006

Closely integrated design is central to the resolution of this combined sports and residential development for Imperial College. The building is situated on a very constrained site in the heart of the Kensington Conservation Area. Planning conditions prioritised a sensitive response to the existing Victorian square and adjacent terraced buildings; a requirement that is reflected in the rhythm of the discrete modern façade. The rear of the building is also profiled to minimise overshadowing of the nearby properties, without compromise to the sports function.

The constraints of the surrounding urban fabric were compounded by a requirement to retain an existing basement pool and squash courts, along with a series of piled foundations designed for a larger building in the same location. These restrictions set the parameters for the new building; which required a unified architectural, building services and structural engineering solution to minimise the impact of the challenging site.

The design takes full advantage of the unusual complexities of the site to provide a compact series of interlocking spaces. These include a multi-purpose hall, five badminton courts and a climbing wall, all designed for simultaneous use; a reception and café; a fitness centre; and an aerobics studio. New components added above the existing building included 12 private apartments for use by Imperial College. These are spread throughout the top three levels of the scheme, and have separate reception and access.

Above
The façade discretely reflects the rhythm of the surrounding Kensington Conservation Area

Right
The site fronts on to Princes Gardens, a verdant Victorian square

The empty site is a void, a missing tooth
To the northern corner of the square

The building programme is complex
Swimming pool, gym, dance studio, residential apartments

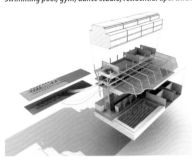

Move away from noisy, vibrant Exhibition Road
And one discovers something altogether different:
Princes Gardens – a generous, green London square

181

Arup Associates Unified Design

Right
Ramped access from street level

The ground is restricted
The parts are arranged from bottom up
A vertical skewer

There is a necessary twist.
Above, the form is tight and compact
The structural frame is efficient.
But travelling to the ground, a side step and shuffle are required
To meet the existing basements

We resist temptation for the façade of the
    building to speak too loudly.
It mediates between the building's inner vibrancy
and the external calmness of the square.
Contemporary, yet quietly resonating with the past
The square is completed

182

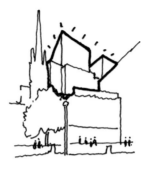

A building form shaped by the city and layers of history
This is no totem object.
A form that evolves from the medieval plan.
A form that belies its enormous scale.
A form shape shifting to circumstance and opportunity.
A form that is only understood in our mindscape through the
*   collaged views experienced from the ground.*
Reconstructed as a coherent whole

Plantation Place

City of London, UK
2004

Above
Shattered glass fins refract and reflect light in the internal atrium

Plantation Place is in the heart of the City of London where it occupies almost a complete block. As with its neighbour, Plantation South, the design of the building reflects a desire to maintain the human scale and complexity of this part of London; and to provide an ecologically efficient, adaptable and healthy workplace.

The massing envelope was shaped by historic Rights of Light agreements and by a response that reflects the different planning requirements for the City skyline and the streetscape below. Beneath the ground, the rich Roman heritage of the area restricted development too: here, an agreement with the City Archaeologist limited the extent of excavation to defined areas, beyond which the ground had to remain undisturbed.

In response to its context, the lower levels of the building reflect the character of the surrounding streets. To maintain these street lines, the floor plates of the building extend to the site boundary. Usefully, this creates deep plan office areas ideal for financial trading operations. The streets around the site are relatively narrow so the façades are designed to be viewed obliquely. Projecting limestone fins create an impression of solidity when viewed obliquely. They also provide a sense of human scale without reducing the occupants' external views.

The fabric of the building changes at mid level, where the structure rises away from the street. At this higher elevation, improved air quality allows a mixed mode ventilation strategy which permits fresh air to be drawn in from outside. The façade is a clear glazed double skin. Opening windows are located in the inner skin. The outer skin protects these opening windows from wind and rain penetration.

The double-skin façade extends to the upper levels of the building. Here the orthogonal floor plates are resolved volumetrically as two distinctive glass cubes, their presence on the City skyline identifying Plantation Place in its wider urban context.

We sought to create an illusion.
A paradox.
Two buildings in one.
One ground hugging;
One re-inventing itself skywards.
Stone/Glass
Earth/Sky

A footprint on the ground that holds the line.
Defines the edge and marks the territory.
Occupying and constructing the space for movement.
From the solid – tracing footsteps;
Carving the void – the people space.
Splitting the form.
Connecting the footprints

Above
The internal atrium

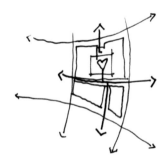

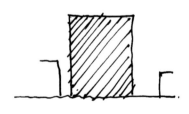

Create the solid

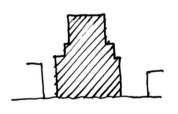

Shape the context

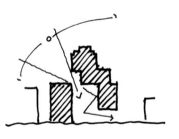

Sculpt the light

Parts of the whole
Connected
Integrated
Unified

Illuminated waterfall: the shattered-glass fins of
the internal atrium act as a light condensor

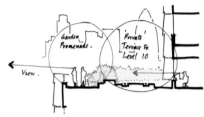

The insertion of Sky Gardens
Creates an alternative urban -scape.
Free of noise, less intense:
Thinking, breathing space
Still connected to the city.
Walk in the sky

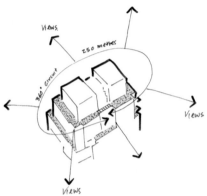

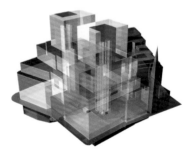

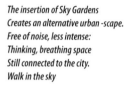

Above
Project components

Above
In this dense urban environment, people-centred open-air sky gardens are an unusual feature of the upper levels

Ropemaker
City of London, UK
Completion 2009

The unusual use of glass and colour, and an extensive collaboration with light sculptors and artists, are a feature of both the interior and exterior of Ropemaker. This is a high quality office and retail environment, driven by an enlightened client with a well established ethos of highly sustainable, flexible, contemporary workplaces.

The project is conceived as a simplified Chinese puzzle where the sum of the parts defines the whole. The building is composed of six large-scale interlocking cubic forms that rise up as a series of garden terraces. These roof terraces are both a remarkable natural amenity for the people who occupy the building and a biodiverse habitat for flora, fauna, insects and birds. The soft landscape is designed to be visible, particularly from the long distance northern views.

The design aims to enhance the relationship of Ropemaker to Moorgate and the larger City buildings beyond, while still respecting the domestic scale of Islington. When buildings of this magnitude are inserted into an existing urban setting, they benefit from façade treatments that minimise their apparent volume. Here this is achieved by modelling the interlocking cubic forms, with careful consideration of the play of light and shade created by the movement of the sun. Additionally, the perceived scale is reduced by articulating and animating the large surfaces. Groups of projecting windows form an overlaid pattern of differential reflection and shadow across the exterior, interlaced with flat, glazed spandrel-panel zones. The colour and rhythmic expression of the façade present a changing canvas of reflectivity and tone, while the projecting arrays also provide additional solar shading.

*Our ambition was to speculate; to rediscover
    the potential of glass.
Could it be re-invented as sustainable material:
To meet the demands of low energy performance,
and explore a visual poetry?*

*The surface of the skin is modulated.
Windows tilt and turn away from the sun path
to minimise carbon emissions.*

*Expansive, uninterrupted floors connect
    in interlocking volumes
To redefine the silhouette on the skyline*

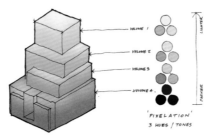

*Artist Antoni Malinowski collaborated
    to create a colour concept.
Inspired by colour layering found in historical
    oil painting techniques,
the skin is made up of a series of glass layers
that modify the appearance of an
    encapsulated pure colour panel:
Analogous to paint application evolved by old masters,
Where translucent glaze layers were used
    to modify the visual effect
Of a pure under-colour applied to the canvas*

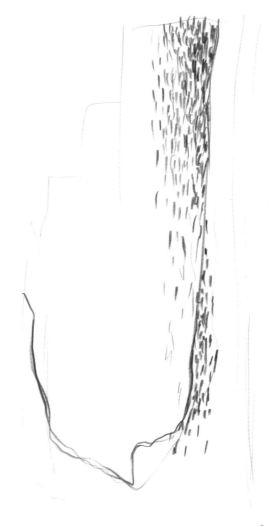

Above
Glass colour treatment concept sketches by artist Antoni Malinowski

Arup Associates Unified Design

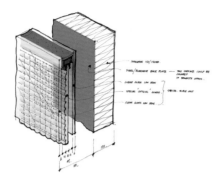

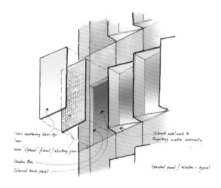

Above
The translucent layering generates a building of subtle polychromatic shifts – a contemporary architecture, resonant with colour

Facing page
Full scale mock-up of the façade window array

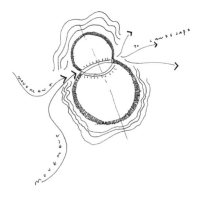

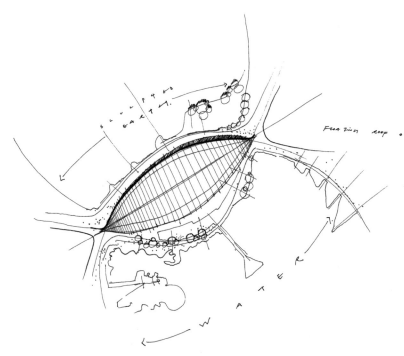

Energy Centre,
Dongtan Eco-City
Dongtan, China
Project 2005

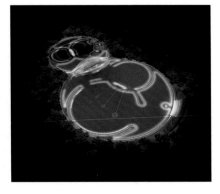

Above
Interlocking circles of the masterplan circumscribe a water
environment and a synthetic landscape

The Energy Centre forms part of the wider eco-city at Dongtan, a new city design that originated with Arup Associates and is now masterplanned by Arup Urban Design. This Chinese city is planned for a population of approximately 500,000 inhabitants – and yet its primary aim is to be carbon neutral. An integrated energy strategy supports the community, a strategy that harnesses a variety of renewable energy sources including biomass, wind, hydro electricity, tidal power and both passive and active solar systems. Environmentally sound food and fuel production and waste disposal methods are all integrated holistically into the energy chain.

The Dongtan Energy Centre is the focus of a major civic park sited centrally within the eco-city. It is located in the heart of the park, which is formed in the shape of two interlocking circles. One circle encloses a natural water environment; the other a manmade synthetic landscape. The building will contain six pavilions, each dedicated to interactive educational exhibitions whose themes expand on the range of alternative energy systems used in the surrounding city.

The skin and roof surfaces that enclose the pavilions exploit a diverse range of traditional and contemporary materials. Taking their cue from nature, bio-mimicry techniques allow the building to respond intuitively to its environment: for example, elements of the roof canopy continuously open and close to encourage natural ventilation.

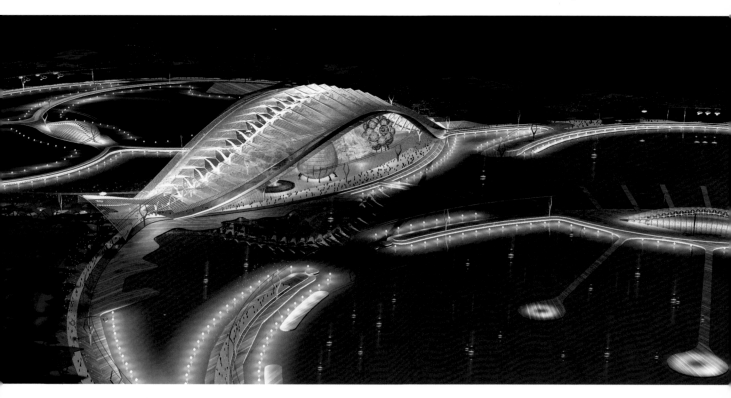

Above
The Energy Centre contains six interactive pavilions themed on the
carbon-neutral energy systems of the surrounding Dongtan City

Below
Concept sketches for the interactive alternative energy pavilions

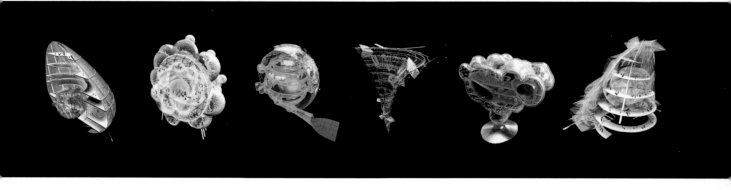

Qintai Art and Cultural Centre
Wuhan, China
Project 2003

Above
Inspiration for the massing of the two buildings was found in
a legendary relationship between two local personalities

This proposal for an art and cultural centre splits the complex into two easily identifiable volumes: a massing that reflects a legendary relationship between two local personalities. The two buildings form a distinct pair; their characters separate and yet complementary. Their position in the landscape is important. The larger volume wears the earth like a cloak, sweeping upwards from the highest point of new terrain to emphasise its verticality; its counterpart occupies a lower position, jutting forward slightly to meet the water.

The larger of the two buildings accommodates the 1,800 seat Grand Theatre, a structure that rises 50 metres above the surrounding ground levels. Its roof void is given over as a viewing platform, from which visitors can pick out the key monuments of the city. The subservient volume is a Concert Hall, 35 metres high and seating 1,600 people; it is a quieter, more enclosed object.

Both buildings are conceived as layered spaces. Voluminous transparent external envelopes clothe the solid performance halls within. The character of these inner performance halls is distinct, and this is reflected in the treatment of materials. The Grand Theatre has staging capabilities that can be easily adapted to the demands of both Chinese and Western productions. It is the more static of the two spaces, and is clad in a sculptured stone surface. The Concert Hall, with acoustic properties that require a more dynamic volume, is characterised by an outer surface of timber.

Top left
A louvred, glazed shroud encloses the two performance volumes

Top right
Detail of the cultural arena within the masterplan

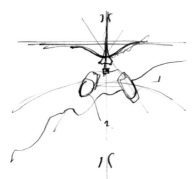

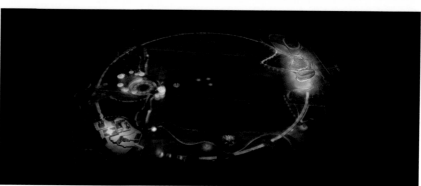

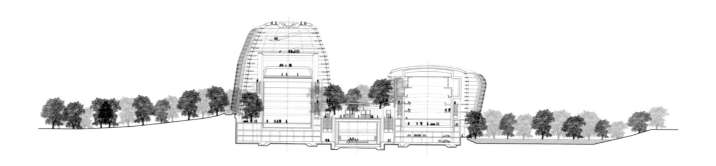

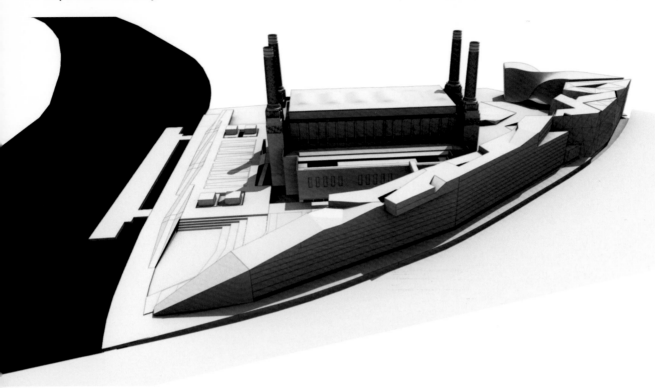

Battersea West Hotel

London, UK

Project 2005

Top
The West Hotel descends towards the Thames to allow views of the Power Station from the river

Right
The Great Wall Walk weaves over and through the West Hotel

Bottom right
Components of the Great Wall Walk: landscape, staircase, sculpted volume and whole

The West Hotel is upside down. The public levels – dramatic spa, restaurants and lobby – are all arranged across the top of the building, strongly expressed as a series of sharply cantilevered volumes that project towards spectacular views of the river and city beyond. The bedrooms are below.

The articulation may be strong, but more important in this environment is the democratic and sensitive urban design strategy that the building characterises. The West Hotel is part of a larger 'wall' of buildings that collectively define the western perimeter of the Battersea Power Station site. They provide a protective edge to the development. But rather than an obstruction, the hotel gradually reduces in height as it approaches the Thames, to reveal sensitive river views of the historic Power Station building.

The enclosing form of the West Hotel is used to create special, wind-sheltered places for people. Not just spaces for hotel users, but for all those who come to this significant London location. Pedestrians are free to use the interconnected sequence of walkways that lace across the surface, from the public gardens to the River Walk.

Unusually, the warping ground plane continues up and over the hotel itself. This is the 'Great Wall Walk' – an inclusive, publicly accessible route across the landscaped roof of the building. The walk 'weaves' directly into the public areas at upper level, and provides extraordinary views over London. This is a strategy that is focussed on design for people. All the public spaces of the site are unified – even those that lie above a normally exclusive luxury hotel.

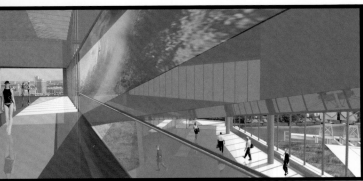

Below
Central concepts of the West Hotel

Right
Public and private routes flow through the West Hotel

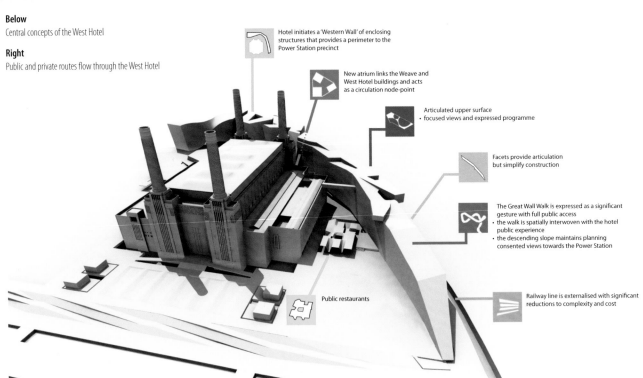

Hotel initiates a 'Western Wall' of enclosing structures that provides a perimeter to the Power Station precinct

New atrium links the Weave and West Hotel buildings and acts as a circulation node-point

Articulated upper surface
• focused views and expressed programme

Facets provide articulation but simplify construction

The Great Wall Walk is expressed as a significant gesture with full public access
• the walk is spatially interwoven with the hotel public experience
• the descending slope maintains planning consented views towards the Power Station

Public restaurants

Railway line is externalised with significant reductions to complexity and cost

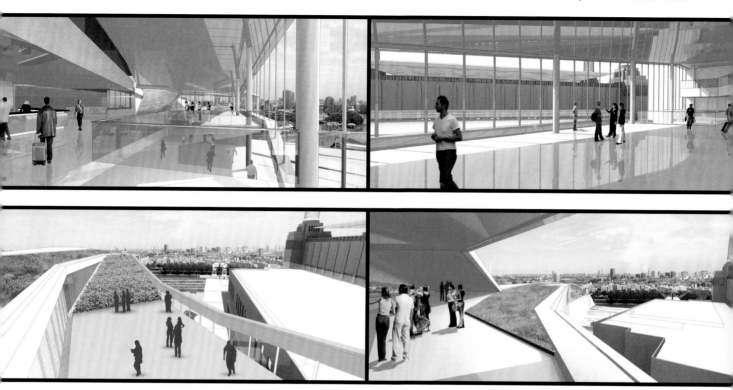

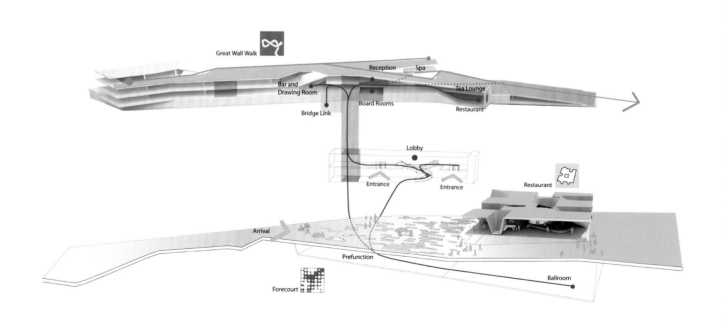

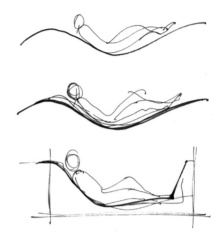

Product Design
Sustainable designs for people

Torni is a new washbasin pod made by the Finnish company Durat. Its basin is made out of moulded 'Durat', a solid polyester thermosetting material containing entirely recycled plastic from industrial sources – one of the few sustainable solid surface materials currently available. The basins are manufactured in a large variety of colours created by combining the finely ground plastic waste with a polymer matrix.

The cylindrical unit departs from traditional horizontal commercial vanity basin design. It originated as a unique solution to a spatially constricted project, where conventional continuous units were impracticable. The shape of the basin increases the sense of space, and users can circulate it comfortably. Recently, the ergonomically comfortable 'Mini Torni' was developed for use by young children in schools and hospitals.

The **Puro Spa Bath** was commissioned by Durat to augment their range of large luxury bathtubs for the domestic and hotel market, in particular to appeal to the growing requirement for a multisensory 'spa bathing' experience. With the concept inspired by the classic profile of Charlotte Perriand 1930s chaise longue, the interior was sensitively moulded to the human form, to provide the most comfortable reclining position. The dimensions were deepened and subtly altered to create a reclined bathing position with curved head support. No water faucet is visible. Instead, water wells up from hidden inlets until it cascades down as a waterfall. When the bath is full, water drawn from the tub circulates to create a constantly flowing stream, visually and aurally reminiscent of a cascading brook.

Again, the product is created from sustainable, recyclable moulded 'Durat'; while the specially designed contour and the re-circulation facility reduce the amount of water required to fill the bath.

Above
Torni washbasin unit

Right
Puro luxury spa bath

The Fourth Plinth Sculpture

Trafalgar Square, London, UK
Ongoing

Unified design is founded on an unusually expansive relationship between the architectural and engineering professions and other creative disciplines. Arup Associates has a long association with the Mayor of London's Fourth Plinth project. The plinth located on the northwest corner of Trafalgar Square was built in 1841 to hold an equestrian statue of William IV, but remained empty due to insufficient funds.

In 1999, the Royal Society of Arts devised the Fourth Plinth Project, which occupied the plinth with a succession of temporary works commissioned from contemporary artists. These included: Mark Wallinger's *Ecce Homo* (1999); Bill Woodrow's *Regardless of History* (2000); and Rachel Whiteread's *Monument* (2001).

The Greater London Authority has continued the series of exhibitions. Shown adjacent is Arup Associates' visualisation of Mark Quinn's poignant figurative work, *Alison Lapper Pregnant* (2005) – a 3.6 metre, 13-ton marble torso-bust of artist and phocomelia sufferer Alison Lapper, who was born with no arms and shortened legs. More recently Thomas Schutte's *Model for a Hotel* (2007) was unveiled.

In each case Arup Associates has directly supported the artists in the physical realisation of their sculptural ambitions; and has also been responsible for negotiating the planning applications on behalf of the RSA and the GLA. Arup Associates continues its relationship with the artists of this project, now as a commissioner within the Fourth Plinth Group.

Right Marc Quinn's *Alison Lapper Pregnant* (2005)

Picture Credits

Acknowledgements

A deep gratitude is owed to a unique community of individuals: the people of Arup Associates. This work reflects the collective power of their shared vision.

The editor and Arup Associates wish to thank executive commissioning editor Helen Castle of John Wiley and Sons, with whom this book found its origin in a conversation in St John's, London, in 2006. She and her team – development editor Mariangela Palazzi-Williams and copy editor Lucy Isenberg – have nurtured and clarified an unruly vision with remarkable patience and tact. Thanks too to collaborators Gary Lawrence, Jonathan Glancey, Jay Merrick, Juhani Pallasmaa, Herbert Girardet, and Leon van Schaik for their lucid and insightful contributions; and to Laura Iloniemi, who from the outset wove together the personalities that created this venture.

Christian Richters is the originator of the majority of the beautiful and inspirational photographs – particularly those of Plantation Lane, Vauxhall Transport Interchange, and the Druk White Lotus School; while Graham Brandon has provided the evocative textural images of Ladakh that interlace the chapters. Finally, this project could not have been completed without the creativity, skill and dedication of the Arup Associates production team – graphic designers Nik Browning and Philip Jones; research assistants Rebecca Harris and Amy Lindsay; and producer Joanne Ronaldson – to all of whom the editor is indebted.

Arup Associates
2000–08

Nicola Adams
Olivia Adderley
Ann Marie Aguilar
Fathima Ahmed
Gert Andresen
Simon Anson
Jake Armitage
Janet Ashong-Lamptey
Rachel Atthis
Thomas Bailey
Sebastiano Baldan
Graeme Bardsley-Smith
Simon Barnes
Mike Beaven
Colin Begg
Twahaa Begum
Ari Bellahsen
Rachel Bennett
Jo Blackburne
Yomi Bola
Michelangelo Bonvino
Andrew Boughton
Gabrielle Bowe
George Bowman
James Bown
Gavin Braidley
Janelle Brathwaite
Anita Bramfit
Paul Brislin
Peter Brittain
Stewart Brooks
Tony Broomhead
Rachel Brown
Nik Browning
Mick Brundle
Eric Budzisz
Joseph Burton

Ian Camilleri
Tristram Carfrae
Glen Carney
Filippo Cefis
Joel Chappell
Kenny Chong
Michal Ciomek
Jason Clark
Monica Clark
Steven Clarke
Chris Clifford
Vincent Cloete
Gavin Cockburn
Deidre Coleman
Charlotte Collas
Angelle Collings
Carl Collins
Rocio Conesa Sanchez
Peter Connell
Lauren Cooke
David Cornwell
Rob Courser
Sarah Crabtree
Natalie Crosman
Sho Das-Munshi
Christina David
Rob Davies
Tony Day
Philip De Neumann
James Devine
Paul Dickenson
Phil Dixon
Mike Dodd
Rory Donald
Fiona Donaldson
John Driskel
John Edgar

Melissa Edmands
Heledd Edwards
Mike Edwards
CJ Elgun
Ramsey Ellenany
Chris English
Christine Evans
Geoff Farnham
Stuart Fenwick
Adam Ferguson
Tanya Ferrara
Martin Finch
Neale Fionda
Lydia Firminger
Alan Foster
Jason Fraiser
Pietro Franconiero
Jason Fraser
Kenneth Fraser
Francesca Galeazzi
Carolyn Gallehawke
Andrew Gardiner
Richard Gargaro
Penny Garrett
Stephanie Gauthier
Michelle Georgens
Marjan Gholamalipour
Graham Gibbon
Peter-John Gilbert
Diane Gilchrist
Tughela Gino
Maureen Godbold
Darren Goodman
Graham Goymour
Ian Grace
Wendy Grant
Rowland Griffin

Becky Griffiths
Hayley Gryc
Rory Gullan
Alejandro Gutierrez
Philippa Hadfield
Martin Hall
Sarah Hall
Kieran Hannon
Hugo Hardy
Tom Hardy
Jackie Harris
Rebecca Harris
Andrew Harrison
Raewyn Harrison
Clare Hart
Rachel Hart
Katrina Hartley
Andy Hau
Alan Hay
Ian Hazard
Toria Hickman
Juliet Ho
Ed Hoare
Tony Hoban
Thomas Honeyman
Lee Hosking
Rob Houmoller
Alastair Hughes
Erin Hunt
Sarah Hunt
David Hymas
Mathieu Jacques De Dixmude
Rachel James
Charlotte Jansingh
Luke Jarvis
Jacqueline Jiang-Haines
Lindsay Johnston

Philip Jones
Richard Jones
Hyuk Jung
Mario Kaiser
Verolucy Kaseri
Ivan Kaye
Vince Keating
Daniel Kelly
Smita Khanna
Rod Kiely
Caroline King
Jason King
Mike King
Michael Kinney
Astrid Korvink
Nadine Koschke
Marek Kowalski
Joey La
John Lacey
Liz Laker
Joanne Larmour
Alistair Law
Andrew Lawrence
Pablo Lazo
Benny Lee
David Lee
Dick Lee
Tommy Lee
Ruth Lees
Stephen Leonard
Matthias Lerch
Clive Lewis
Suzanne Li
Benjamin Lim
Eduarda Lima
Amy Lindsay
Robert Lisle

Peter Llewellyn
Bee Choo Lloyd
Michael Lowe
Sean Macintosh
Julia Malewski
Caroline Marklew
Teresa Marshall
David Martin
Helen Massy-Beresford
Paul Matthews
Chris McAnneny
Gary McCarthy
Richard McCarthy
Will McLardy
Peter McLaughlin
Martina McManus
Stephanie McNabb
Daryl Miles
John Miles
Edoardo Milli
Britta Misdalski
Andrew Moise
Marek Monczakowski
Fanwi Monie
Claire-Louise Moore
Braulio Morera
Tom Morgan
Marianne Morris
Nigel Morris
Hannah Morrison
John Napier
Nevine Nasser
Shahzad Nazir
Owain Nedin
Emily Norman
Declan O'Carroll
Bethany O'Brien

Henry O'Kello
Rebecca O'Neill
Chantel Operman
Sherman Ou
Kevin Owens
Mark Oxbrough
Kuljinder Pank
David Parsons
Dipesh Patel
Kantaben Patel
Jacek Pazdzior
David Pearce
Annelise Penton
Nicola Perandin
Antonio Perez
Keith Perry
Paulo Pimentel
George Podoski
Lizzie Pomeroy
Geoff Powell
Georgina Price
Robert Pugh
Julia Quarry
Terry Raggett
Aminur Rahman
Stephen Ratchye
Graham Redman
James Reed
Patrick Regan
Roland Reinardy
Mark Richardson
Constance Ridout
John Roberts
Andrew Robertson
Laura Robertson
Michelle Robinson
Susan Rolfe

Joanne Ronaldson
Davina Rooney
Jonathan Rose
Alan Ross
Swati Salgaocar
Nicola Sanderson
Rob Saunders
Ken Sayer
Brendan Scarborough
Haico Schepers
Timm Schoenberg
Daniel Schwaag
George Scott
Eeling See
Stephen Setford
Elizabeth Shaw
Melody Shi
Cate Sirkett
Luke Smeaton
Adam Smith
Malcolm Smith
Matthew Smith
Sara Smith
Stephanie Smith
Tina Smythe
Tim Snelson
Nikolaos Socratous
Caroline Sohie
Susie Srebric
Stephen Stanley
David Stevens
Geoff Stevens
Lexy Stevens
Callum Stewart
Lee Stidolph
Eric Sturel
Peter Sullivan

Alex Summerfield
Nick Suslak
Julie Talbot-Dunn
Alan Tang
Jeff Teerlinck
Alan Thompson
Mike Thomson
Gareth Thyer
Danielle Tinero
Gino Tughela
William Turena
Jade Turner
Robert Updegraff
Eugene Uys
Clarissa Van Der Putten
Mark Van Lith
Eduard Van Zyl
Lee Vanacher
Ray Vincent
Cara Von-Simson
Max Walker
Dave Wall
Malcolm Wallace
Juliet Walshe
Peter Warburton
James Ward
Hayley Wards
Sally Ware
Adamu Waziri
Stewart Weathers
Gary Webb
Jeanne Webber
Dan Weekes
David Westcott
Marcus Weyler
Susie Whitamore
Hayley Williams

Nick Williams
Pam Williams
Ralph Wilson
Ken Wiseman
Marcin Wojewski
Joanne Wolbers
Daniel Wong
Jonathan Wong
Katie Wood
Roger Wood
Tim Worsfold
Jonathan Yeung
Hitoshi Yonamine
Vincent Young